'NO SPEAK ENGLISH'

A journey of migration and resistance

'NO SPEAK ENGLISH'

A journey of migration and resistance

Tara Mistry

Front cover: Tara and her two brothers, Suresh and Chandra

Back cover: Suresh, Mum, Tara and Chandra

© Tara Mistry (2025)

Dedication

This book is dedicated to all my family members who feature in this account, especially my brothers; thank you for allowing me to bring our story (albeit from my perspective) to our wider family and audience. I am sure your interpretations and accounts would differ. I hope you will share key themes and narratives, and hopefully this will give you opportunities to explore your own stories with your children and families. Please forgive any inaccuracies or misinterpretations. There are bound to be some, but they are my interpretations and recollections.

Thank you to all my friends who have encouraged me over the years to write this account and those who bought me books and resources to keep me motivated.

Above all this is my homage to Bapuji (Dad) who made many sacrifices for us and died too young to see the fruits of his labour, and to Ba (Mum), who has survived many challenges in her life and at 91 has lived over 62 years in a foreign land, now very much her home.

We held a 90th birthday celebrations for Mum in Leicester in December 2023. All her children, their partners, nearly all her grandchildren with their partners and her great grandchildren were present. In my speech about her life, I hope I spoke for my family as I concluded:

'Ba, your very multi racial and diverse family are forever grateful for all your resilience and support and your ability to adapt to the changing world around us with courage, wisdom, faith and understanding.

We would not be here without you.'

Acknowledgements

My immense gratitude and heartfelt thanks to two women who have given up an immeasurable amount of time at different stages of this writing process.

The first, Claire Wintram, read my first rough draft and helped me see the 'wood from the trees' and gave me the initial encouragement by her enthusiasm for the stories. The second is Hilary Burgess, who has edited the near final drafts with her skill and sensitivity to help me do justice to my family's past and present.

And lastly, many thanks to Roger Carnt, who kindly offered to support me to the printing stage of this book.

I am indebted to all three.

Peter: Thank you for being that steady 'rock' in our lives, the true meaning of your name.

Nalini and Sunita: Thank you for inspiring me to write.

The present is where we get lost-
if we forget our past and have no vision of the future
Ayi Kwei Armah, The Healers (1978)

Contents

Introduction 1

PART 1: Early 1900s – 1962 7

    Navsari family 8

    Munsad family 21

    Kenya years 33

    Family return to India 39

    Dad in Kenya then England 42

    The Munsad years 45

    Ready to leave India 59

PART 2: 1963 – 1974 66

    Early days in Leicester 67

    Playtime and leisure 77

    Early education 87

    Food and shops 93

    Dad's stroke 96

    Living with Dad's disability 101

    Secondary school 104

    Dad's final days and after 111

    Sixth-form and onwards 122

PART 3: Post 1974 and beyond 130
    Our changing lives 131
    Higher education: new horizons and parallel lives ... 136
    Graduation and leaving home 143
    My brothers' marriages 146
    Becoming a professional probation officer 153
    Joining the Labour Party: politics and activism 155
    Back to India, 21 years on 157
    Settling in Bristol 171
    From home to seeking asro at ASRA 176
    Health and reframing Mum's life 185
Glossary 195

Introduction

I have been writing this 'memoir/social history' of my family and our migration for so long that I have lost whole chapters of it over the years. When I first started, we were not even using computers. Various notebooks were used, discarded, or forgotten. I had kept hard copies, so it has been interesting to revisit my earlier missives which were raw and reflected distinct stages of my life. In fact, at various points I abandoned the project because certain incidents were upsetting (although quite therapeutic), and it meant the project was postponed for a long time. There were also life events, work and family pressures and ill health which often got in the way. But in truth, authoring a story which is about family is exceedingly difficult. Describing the process of migration and becoming part of the diaspora; leaving loved ones and cultural connections; forming new relationships in a new country; experiencing the savage racism of the 60's and early 70's; growing up in relative poverty and trying to make a new life is always going to be difficult to reflect upon. Describing family dynamics and writing about people who are still alive mean there is an added responsibility to be careful. How they feel about what I write - that might not synchronise with their perceptions and recollections - is an important consideration.

After forming and reforming this account over successive periods of my life and now arriving to some kind of completion for sharing, it now feels daunting. But it needs to be shared at some point. I hope this account is more rounded with the rawness of the earlier drafts more tempered. Of course, that may mean it is more sanitised and reflective as opposed to 'telling it like it is.' But what is telling it like it is?

It can only be my interpretation of our family history, albeit clarified with stories and recollection of other members to a degree. I did get stories and recollections from my Mum, and she provided a treasure trove of her early life; some stories I could remember her telling us over the years. I did conduct early interviews with my brothers, and they were useful and are incorporated here. Later, I tried interviews and creating templates for them to reflect and respond to, but despite reminders these were not forthcoming. I was trying to gather insights from their perspectives. As we lived long distances from each other, and life got in the way, it was hard to do more than occasionally cajole. To be fair to my brothers, they were possibly ambivalent about what I was going to cover and how open and explicit I was going to be. It is true that despite having experienced things in common we would have different recalls and interpretations. I have tried to be careful with stories but also wanted to get into the cultural and social changes taking place within my family and my community over time.

We are a vastly different family now to the one that migrated. Is that due to the impact of migrating to a western country, and/or social changes resulting from education and especially higher education for women? Or is it our own communities adapting, with opportunities for employment and careers outside the home, or the migrant communities themselves evolving? Or is it a combination, affected by the developments of wider society, and of course the rise of social media and technology. It is hard to be specific although my observations of new migrant communities in Britain do show similar themes of adaptation, or a mixture, but retaining our distinct cultures.

After many years grappling with the family history (especially from our time in England) and trying to get some ideas of those shared experiences I realised it must be *my* story, and as such I interpreted it through my lens of an aspiring feminist who saw things from a race, class, and gender perspective. It is important to be clear about this at the outset as this is what makes it different from, for example, my brothers writing it. My interpretation is influenced by all of this, and my own experiences and observations. This account, like a lot of memoirs and oral history are my take on our history and although I try to be objective, there is bound to be subjectivity by the lens from which I choose to observe. Also, interpretations of the past are influenced by the present. It is important to stress that this is not a detailed family ancestry, and I have not undertaken formal research to that effect. As with all memoirs and oral history not all stories or relationships get equal treatment and so I hope the general themes will cover the salient points I try to convey.

People asked who was I writing this for? Initially it was for my daughters to have a record of the history of our Indian family and to give them a glimpse of the lives of their maternal grandparents and great-grandparents whose lives were so different to anything they could imagine. I wanted them to understand what migration meant for me, my parents, and my brothers. Over the years, the focus changed to incorporate more of the social history and change that I wanted to capture for a wider audience, including my family, friends and the wider Prajapati community in Britain and those who migrated over many parts of the world in the last fifty or sixty years. It is in part a story about 'mother – daughter' relationships, and in my case how these change and evolve over the course of our lives.

From an early age, I was able to understand the socio-political context of societies and gendered roles more clearly than many of my white and Indian friends - especially in our family structures. The political context of power dynamics and wider debate in early 1970's Britain also influenced me. Another notable impact was the role of television in the early to late 1960's. The TV was in its infancy, still with only two to three channels, but to us from an Indian village, it was a magic box. It offered me a gateway to information and knowledge.

My Dad was always keen on us watching the BBC News. I watched news about the Black Civil Rights struggle in America on our TV screens, and it gave me an early understanding of racism and an early awareness of injustice, inequality, and the role of politics. The coverage on the news of CND and marches in those early days later led me to support women at Greenham Common, and to lifelong opposition to nuclear arms. Inequality and injustice and poverty were portrayed through TV dramas such as 'Cathy Come Home', 'Edna the Inebriate Woman', 'Saturday Night Sunday Morning', and later series like 'Shoulder to Shoulder' (with Sian Phillips portraying Emmeline Pankhurst) on the history of the suffragettes. These were to help me make sense of a patriarchal world, and later I explored women's role in society more broadly through my university studies in social sciences and a professional qualification in Social Work and through the Women's Liberation Movement. By the time I was fourteen, I had signed up to be a member of the Campaign Against Racial Discrimination (CARD). I was an avid reader of Dickens and devoured his books because of the centrality of an underdog (particularly a child) rising above what people expected of them. I read about women such as Amelia Urquhart and Elizabeth Backwell, the first woman doctor, to give me hope and inspiration about what was possible to achieve as a woman. So, it is important for readers to understand that this history is influenced by those early experiences and by the fact that I was an Indian girl who was unhappy in the gendered role that my family and community imposed. At the time, it was even more constrained than the patriarchal role of women in wider society in Britain.

I am also a product of a Eurocentric educational system that paid little attention in history to the role of Britain as an imperial power that had colonised vast parts of the world, including India, Africa, and the Caribbean as part of the Commonwealth. We only started to understand the concept *'we are here because you were there'* much later. That notion - that we migrated because of the link Britain had with our homeland - only became clearer once we became older. It is only now that the curriculum in schools is addressing the Transatlantic Slave Trade. However, the role of Asian and Black soldiers in two World Wars and Britain's colonial past in respect of India and the wider subcontinent are still inadequately addressed in Britain. The issues surrounding the Partition of India and its consequences have only recently been articulated and explored via the media. As far as I am aware, these are not subjects taught in the school curriculum as yet.

So, those of us who are products of the 1960's and 1970's primary to higher education were learning from a very biased Eurocentric model. As a result, my heroes and heroines were white, and culturally I was drawn to be one of those aspirational white women about whom I was often reading. It was hard to understand why that was always going to be difficult!

I came later to the struggles of Black and Asian women through the Trade Union movement (for example, strikes at Imperial Typewriters and at Grunwick) where the majority workers were South Asian, with Jayaben Desai playing a leading role in defending the rights of migrant workers. Books like Amrit Wilson's 'Finding a Voice' and Buchi Emecheta's 'In the Ditch' in the 1970's and early 1980's were significant influences for me. Nowadays, there is so much in the fiction and non-fiction literature from Black authors and increasingly large numbers of Asian (and specifically Indian writers) from the diaspora. It feels more positive for young Asian people to see their lives represented better in all areas of society and not to feel that they need to be inhabiting a white skin to find a place in the world. I know it is still a challenge, and we are not there yet. But unfortunately, many of us did internalise that way of thinking to progress as young people growing up in the Britain of that era with very few Black/Asian role models.

I hope this is more than just a memoir but also a social history, which illuminates and illustrates the changing diverse nature of Britain and the position of our community of Gujarati Prajapatis that came in the late 1950's and early 1960's. This period was well before the arrival of East African Asians in the 1970's. Some of these, who were our relatives, came with a lot more in terms of education and qualifications, and were more likely to be middle class than the early groups that included our family. Although we had a connection with Kenya by virtue of our birth, our experience was that of rural migrants from Gujarat, India. We were forming a community with people who were from a similar background but from a wider pool of India and the subcontinent than just Gujarat.

When we arrived in Leicester in January 1963, the 'Asian community' included friends and relatives who coalesced with others from Hindu, Muslim and Sikh religions. There was a sense of us being visible minorities shaped more than by the colour of our skin - also by our religion, culture, language, the clothes we wore and the values we had in common. We were a smaller number then, so there was a sense of solidarity across the diverse group. This has changed, especially in a city like Leicester, where people originally from the Indian subcontinent outnumber the 'host community', and religious affiliation, caste and class has taken on more importance as various Asian communities and subgroups transfer from the status of migrants to British Asians.

I have added a Glossary which might help the readers navigate family relationships and the terminology used to describe them.

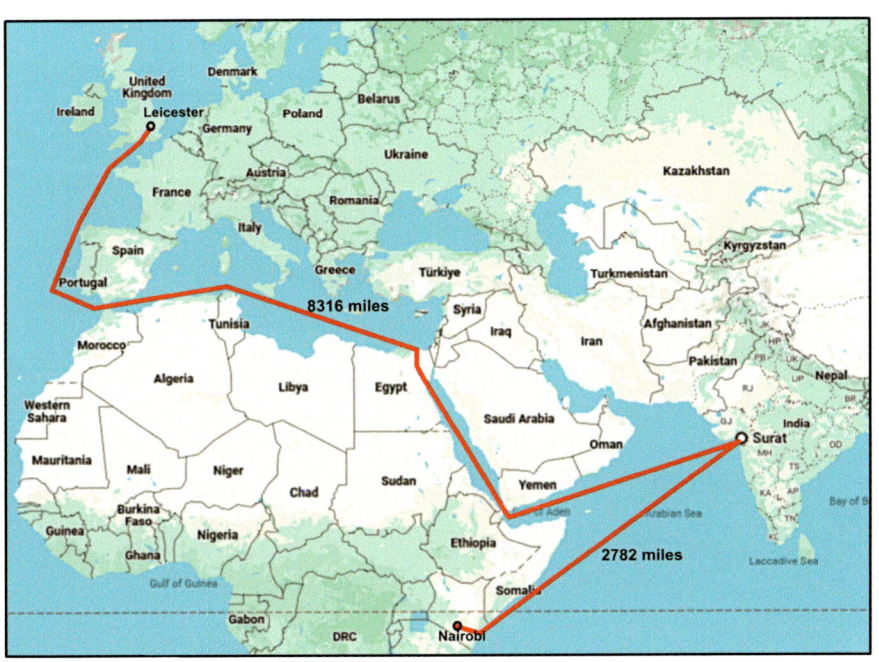

PART 1: Early 1900s – 1962

In this Part I start with the overview and background of my Mum's side of her family in Navsari. I then move to an overview and background of my Dad's side of the family in the village of Munsad, both in the District of Surat, Gujarat, and about 5 miles apart.

I cover my parents' marriage and subsequent few years in Kenya when my Mum joined Dad. This is followed by the birth of my two brothers Suryakant (Suresh), Chandrakant (Chandra) and myself Taramati (Tara), and our move back to India.

My Dad's move to England via Kenya followed whilst we stayed behind in Munsad for five and a half years with my paternal grandmother (Laduma) and my aunt (known to us as Bhulima, my Dad's widowed sister- in-law).

I cover our preparation for joining Dad in England, our journey on the P&O cruise ship *SS Stratheden* from Bombay (now Mumbai) on 24th December 1962 arriving in England on 12th January 1963. In history books this is known as the 'big freeze' and one of the coldest and snowiest winters on record, lasting until March 1963. The catalyst for the move at that that time is likely to have been Dad's fear of the impact of the Commonwealth Act of 1962 preventing us from joining him in England.

Navsari family

My Ajima (Kuvarben) came from a wealthy family and her paternal grandfather, Ratanjbhai, was a respected ayurvedic practitioner. The family had a construction and brick-making company. Ajima's mother, Diwaliben (my great Ajima), had been married and widowed young and had a son, Morarbhai, who was known as a 'cripple' and sadly referred to by that name. In those days women in our Prajapati caste family who were widowed young or divorced were able to get remarried with intervention from families. This was not so in other higher caste communities. It was a practical solution to be able to provide for the young family.

Great Ajima would have been considered a catch with a son, but a disabled son could have hindered her chances for a future marriage. Morarbhai had a limp and could not walk easily. However, it was arranged and Great Ajima ended up marrying into the family and went on to have two more sons and three daughters. They were Gopalbhai, Chaganbhai, Paliben, Bhikhiben and Kuvarben (my Ajima). Gopalbhai was also disabled. Growing up we had contact with my Ajima's siblings and remember both of Mum's disabled mamas (uncles). The stigma and discrimination for disabled people and their families in Indian society was harsh, and so as children we were very conscious of these things. Mum's uncle, Chaganmama, was not particularly nice to my Ajima in those days, but his daughters Shanti and Pushpa (Mum's cousins) ended up in Coventry, so they became quite important and loved relatives when we all settled in the Midlands, England.

Ajima, was officially 'married off' at the age of two to my Ajabapa (Ravjibhai), aged five. This is curious because her older sisters were not married off so young and my Ajima was the youngest and would usually have been married even later. My Mum believes that there was selfishness on the part of her own Ajima in wanting to keep their youngest daughter near them. It is very unusual because girls of any generation from Hindu communities like ours are seen on marriage as belonging to their husband's family, and in early 1918 when Ajima was born, that certainly would have been the case. The parents would hold the children on their laps and an official ceremony of marriage would take place. My Ajima returned to live at home with her own parents. She would be taken to her in-law's family from time to time but would not live with her husband, my Ajabapa, until she had reached puberty, which was about the age of fourteen. It always intrigued me as to why my Ajima was married off into a family that were on all accounts very violent and chaotic. Ajabapa's families were certainly not wealthy, or even comfortable, but it was likely they would have been considered quite desirable when the toddlers were united. It seems that Ranchod Morar (Mum's paternal great-grandfather), who was married to Nandi, had gone to South Africa as a labourer, as people did in those days. He would have been doing what many did to earn money at that time. But the fact that he had gone abroad to work, however menial the job, would have made his family seem aspirational and so considered a good match for marriage.

The period between the marriage and Ajima being ready to go to live as a proper wife showed that this family had multiple problems and was dysfunctional and violent. Ajabapa was turning into a gambler and an alcoholic, not foreseen when the marriage was agreed. My Ajima's parents became aware of problems with the family as they all lived in the same city and so were exploring a possibility of formal divorce or an annulment for their daughter. This would have been possible if the marriage had not been consummated. But during those periods when my Ajima was visiting and staying with her in-laws' family, my Mum thinks Ajima did fall in love with Ajabapa. I can remember Ajabapa being very handsome and quite a dashing figure – the few photos we have are proof of that. My Ajima felt she would be able to change him and have a positive impact. Unfortunately, over generations women have gone into relationships thinking those very thoughts, and not much seems to have changed on that front to this day. Ajima was pregnant soon after moving into the family home as a wife and argued for her right to stay with Ajabapa and his family. Her parents had no choice but to accept her wishes. They were both incredibly young and no doubt were in love. Ajima was only fifteen when my Mum, Laxmi was born.

Great Ajima realised that my Ajima was particularly good with her deaf brother Gopal, who was referred to as gungamama meaning 'deaf uncle' in Gujarati. Even now people refer to him as that when identifying him.

She would look out for him, and it is likely that great Ajima thought my Ajima would be there for him after she herself had died. Her half-brother, Morar, had been sent to Surat to be an apprenticed woodcarver and so had a skill which was important for employment. Gopal was also a skilled woodcarver – working with the revered sandalwood which was used widely for carvings. Both brothers were married off, their parents having given a dowry in reverse – in effect a price paid to the bride's family for the men's disability. Gopal, considered very bright and gifted, was, I am told, treated badly by his wife. Ajima defended him fiercely, often getting into confrontation with her sister-in-law against the family's treatment of her brother. This lasted all their lives, the sister standing up to a disablist society and wider family. Neither of the other two brothers appeared to have supported Ajima.

Ajima's other sister, Bhiki, was remarkably close to her and they stayed close all their lives. She was married off as an older teenager to a man in South Africa (Bhanabhai). He was a widowed businessperson, and she went on to live and settle in South Africa. They lived vastly different lives to my Ajima, as Bhanabhai had made a lot of money. He might have been a descendant of the original indentured Indian workers who were replacements for former slaves. Many returned to India after indentureship ended, but finding little employment some went back to the colonies, developed skills and became educated. Bhanabhai's family were part of the successive generations of Indians settling in South Africa. Despite the system of apartheid, they participated in business so were affluent, although they were labelled 'coloureds' and were subject to segregation laws under the apartheid system. However, they had a comfortable life materially. They supported my Ajima financially during the difficult years with my Ajabapa, who was increasingly gambling and drinking his money away. They were very much part of our family history and future relationships as, later in England, my Mum in return for their generosity gave support to their son. He came to study medicine in England, as he was prevented from doing so in South Africa due to the apartheid regime, and qualified as a doctor. Mum also helped to find a husband for their daughter, oversaw the wedding and provided a guardian's support to her during my own Dad's illness. In effect 'paying back' for all the things her aunt had done for the family over the years.

Our Hindu family and friends' relationships are often dependent on aap-leh (this means 'give and take') arrangement, implying that you pay back in kind for any good deed that the family does for you. To this day I suffer with feelings of guilt if someone does a favour to me, or contributes financially, and I do not find the opportunity to repay. It is a philosophy of not being indebted, and I have seen it practised nobly (and not so nobly) in my life. In our current British society, there are so many inequalities in all our communities that the principles of aap-leh are often blurred as family members transcend class depending on their economic success and professional status. Across continents and countries, the Indian diaspora still supports families, but with less emphasis on receiving and more on helping financially and practically where possible. In our extended family we have seen my Mum's nephew in Canada support his older brother's children in practical and financial ways. It is more altruistic in the current economic climate and giving a helping hand to close relatives is seen to be important evolution of the aap-leh principles from my observation of my wider family.

Back in the early days in Navsari, my Ajima and Ajabapa were now an established married couple and living in the same town as Ajima's parents (known as piyar). This arrangement (husband living in the same vicinity as the in-laws) was frowned upon by the relatives. It was considered an act of humiliation by the husband's wider family. They stayed in great Ajima's family area in Navsari named Patel Fariya – literally 'Patel area.' They were in a rented house for many years and Ajabapa was often ridiculed by his family for being 'spineless' and conspiring with his wife's family. It was seen as a sign of weakness and not holding his place in society. This was all part of the patriarchal society that in this case worked against the man. Mum recalls hearing that my Ajabapa had gone to his parents' house and was rebuked yet again. He had five brothers and one sister, so the pressure from his brothers must have been immense. They got into a huge physical fight and, according to Mum, Ajabapa's head was 'split open.' He returned home and they bandaged him up. Despite this, they stayed in Patel Fariya until Mum was about ten years old.

After that the family moved to Kumbharwad, the potters' area where Ajabapa's family lived, so considered a more appropriate place for them to live. We come from the Prajapati caste who were artisans, skilled workers, and labourers. Our family were potters, carpenters, woodcarvers, and craftspeople. Marriages had to be within the same caste groups (the practice of endogamy) and families were introduced by relatives and intermediaries who were looking out for a suitable boy or a girl.

To an extent that still happens in our communities and internationally amongst the diaspora over the world. Just consider the modern-day equivalent in Netflix programmes (for example) that show professional wedding fixers in America helping find 'Desi partners' - an arrangement initiated by parents or by the individual's seeking partners. There are websites and apps in Britain providing an introduction for possible marriages. The practice of endogamy is less strictly applied these days and could mean that someone broadly from the Gujarati community is acceptable rather than from the Prajapati caste. The diaspora communities replicate the religion and rituals from the homeland, although they get adapted over time, depending on the country of settlement and with successive generations.

There was lot of macho aggression and bad blood within Ajabapa's family. His brothers Khusal and Jagu were particularly violent bullies in the early days and Mum can remember them beating my Ajima on occasions. This sanction for families to treat the daughter-in-law or sister-in-law with impunity was accepted behaviour and still survives, particularly in rural areas where custom and practice have not been challenged. The 'family systems' become entrenched to a point where successive generations perpetuate the things that had been endured by them earlier in life (using power of seniority, hierarchy and control) by both men and women. Interestingly, Jagubhai had his bride introduced and arranged by my Ajima and, despite the violence, they still undertook tasks for the household. Finding a marital partner was a high-status role so this meant my Ajima must have had good standing in the family hierarchy. She was a bit of a networker and was quite 'savvy' about 'who was who' in the community. I think you could say she had local intelligence of what was going on in the neighbourhood.

My Ajabapa was called Ravjibhai. His real name was Parsottam, but he was known as Ravji as he was born on Sunday (Ravi is the Gujarati word for Sunday). Male names usually had their father's name attached (the equivalent would be 'son of') so he was known as Ravi Ranchod. He was the eldest child born in 1915, and his siblings were Khusalbhai, Narsibhai, Ramiben, Ganjiben, Jagubhai and Govindbhai. So, there were seven children on Ajabapa's side, five boys and two girls. Not much is known about the family except that Khusal and Narsi, the two brothers, married two sisters. As children in India, we did not have much to do with Ajabapa's family, but we had quite a bit of contact with his brother Jagubhai (we called him Jagubapa) and his family whilst in England. This was because he too went to Africa, and while in Mombasa wrote a letter to my Dad asking to borrow money as he was planning to come to England and was seeking funds to pay for his passage. The letter was written in the late 1950's and Mum read this to me recently when she was throwing away old airmail letters. My Dad might have been in England and was saving to send for us. Dad was an honourable man and offered £20 which was equivalent to 3-4 weeks of his wages. He always believed we had to help each other out as best we could if a family member made a request. This was also accepted aap-leh relationship; although you could never guarantee a return, people tried to help family members especially if it helped elevate them to a better life. So, despite Jagubapa's early days and his behaviour to my Ajima, the relationships changed for the better once he eventually ended up in England.

Jagubapa also mellowed as he migrated, married, and had his own family. But in those earlier days in India, the relationships were not good with Jagubapa and my grandparents. Migration, and the arrival of the next generation improved relationships; this is quite understandable as our lives with relatives were more interdependent in England. His sons were particularly respectful of my Mum and Dad, and they had a good relationship with each other in England. The bonds of the family or even villages carried onto our new lives bound by values, culture, and religious beliefs of our communities. In many cases (and particularly so with this relationship and our Coventry relatives) any bad blood did not continue in England and especially with the newer generations.

Connections to family and kin become particularly important during migration to a foreign land, especially for those coming from the Indian sub-continent to the 'West'.

My own Ajabapa and Ajima went on to have nine children (four daughters and five sons) with my mum being the eldest. In order, Laxmiben, Maganbhai, Dhaiben, Champackbhai, Manekbhai, Padmaben, Kantubhai, Ramilaben and Kishorbhai. This youngest uncle (our Kishormama) is the same age as my older brother Suresh and was born while my parents were in Kenya. So, my Ajima and my Mum were having babies at the same time.

Back in the early days in India, Mum's family were living in extreme poverty in a densely packed neighbourhood, with Ajabapa working sporadically but drinking and gambling at other times. Ajima was constantly exhausted giving birth and coping with the violence and lack of money. Mum remembers looking after her siblings with all that this entailed. Life was rudimentary, and she recalls with much distress and emotion the day when two of her siblings, her sister and brother - Dhai and Champack - died from a childhood disease (probably smallpox) on the same day as the neighbour's three children. Mum is unclear on specific type of 'pox' but before eradication smallpox was a major cause of mortality worldwide with millions of deaths, so very likely to be smallpox. The neighbourhood was in grief at the shock of losing five little lives in one day.

Our Manekmama also had smallpox but survived somehow. Throughout his life he was seen as mando – someone who is constantly in ill health. But, despite this and his limited education, Manekmama went on to do well as he certainly possessed tenacity, single mindedness, and resilience. He worked in the diamond-cutting business, which was a key industry in Navsari and the Surat district in the 1960s, 70's and the 80's. He went on to make money and build a home for the extended family and moved them out of squalor.

However, at the time of Dhai and Champak's death the context was not just poverty and violence, but also the persecution of women, who were scapegoated and blamed. One of the ways the community did this was through spreading rumours about superstition and witchcraft. Often women and mothers were singled out for this treatment and my Ajima was no exception. This was the way that our society behaved. The use of witchcraft and superstition to explain adversity can be observed around the world in poorer countries and beyond. I am often reminded of the Salem Witch trials in the U.S. and similar examples when I think about these events.

The combination of misfortune coupled with ill health, poverty and illiteracy in some communities seems to me to perpetuate scapegoating being used as an 'explanation' for often rational, but unusual outcomes. Ajima was denounced as a dakan at that time as were other mothers experiencing similar incidents. Dakan is a term for a witch, for 'killing her children' and not saving them. Even though smallpox had taken their lives and the lives of the other children on a grand scale across the world, the implication for these mothers was dire. The fact that people could label women as witches was clearly a gendered assault on powerless women. Somehow the men were not accused of such a thing – there was not an equivalent label. It is unbearable to think that with all the grief and stress, both relatives and whole communities were labelling individual women and in effect 'witch-hunting' them. The power to just accuse someone of witchcraft if anything bad was perceived to have happened meant that the accused was left ostracised and totally vulnerable, even within their own families.

On top of this there was often what we would consider 'brutal' practices relating to health and illness. These often worked together with superstition and seem to heap more pain and suffering on top of the natural causes. When my Maganmama had two huge growths in his tummy (which I guess could have been some kind of inflammation) the family could not afford a doctor or hospital fees, so they took him to a 'witch doctor'. They would go to a person known or recommended to cast a few flicks of long feathers over the aggrieved person to cast away the demons (so-called pichi) and render them better. There would be a cost to this and if it did not work the family would take the adult or child to be branded with a hot blade by someone who had set themselves up in this role. Whilst this is clearly seen as child abuse in our modern world, usually the parents or relatives taking the children for these 'treatments' did not want to hurt them but hoped it would cure them. Mum recalls her brother, already in pain, being held down while the 'doctor' branded him with hot flat blades on the two parts of the large growth and used four smaller blades to brand him on the smaller growth. The pain from the growth and then the pain from the physical branding is a form of torture that is hard to fathom. Mum can remember the smell of burning skin. The wound would often fester and there was nothing to ease it; there was a belief that the pus formed was drawing the malady out of the wound. As the eldest sister, my Mum had to help nurse her brother as my Ajima had other children being born or in need of her. It is impossible to imagine her brother's suffering but also her own. Mum cried recounting these stories and my Ajima's plight in trying to bring up her children. I am sure many children and adults died of sepsis and complications from the branding of the skin or from shock. Mum says that later salt solution was applied to seal the wound adding further to the terror and the pain. It is astounding that any children survived their childhood. This branding also happened to his younger brother, Manekmama, who had earlier survived smallpox.

A few years later this was also practised on my eldest brother, Suresh, who had asthma. His branding was much smaller than Maganmama's, but it seems bizarre that people would think this was an act of healing for something which caused him distress but was not life threatening. My brother was no more than six and often breathless. He was in severe distress particularly at night. I cannot remember this happening to him because I was only about two or three. He still has the scar to remind him of those early years, and it is hard to think he had to endure that as a small boy. He was genuinely loved, and it was meant to make him better rather than as a punishment. However, it is 'treatment' based on ignorance and no doubt satisfied the needs of some sadists that practised it and made money out of this superstition. It maybe that some of these 'practitioners' genuinely believed it was a cure for the illness. Later in England, Suresh was helped by medication until he reached his mid-50s when his asthma stopped - as did his medication. His childhood was marred by it even in England but fortunately he is generally very healthy in his older years.

Seeing and hearing these stories made me question religion and all its manifestations as this practice was confused with religion especially in rural peasant villages. Meanwhile the whole family suffered. Dad was not in India at the time, but I am sure would not have allowed it as, although not highly educated, he did not have time for superstition or religious zealotry. He was a rational man and did not suffer fools gladly and would have dismissed these 'practitioners'. In discussing this with my brother in recent years he does not recall it so well and feels sympathy for parents who felt compelled to do something in the absence of any clear clinical advice or a free and independent health service. Middle-class and rich people in India were obviously able to pay for professional healthcare. Poorer people did not know what else to do to improve or relieve ill-health in their children in villages in the 1950's and even now this kind of intervention for illness and disease is practised.

Ajima's life consisted of having one child after another. Ajabapa was successfully working as carpenter (suthar) when he was sober. There were some opportunities for him to find a way to make a living, but sadly he could not sustain any jobs for long and continued a pattern of periods of drinking and working intermittently. There was no regular income, as even when Ajabapa worked the money would go on alcohol. As well as caring for the needs of her disabled brothers (who were both very dependent on her) my Ajima was dealing with regular childbirth and poverty, and an alcoholic husband. At an incredibly early age, my uncles (mamas) would be sent out to look for my Ajabapa in any place he might have collapsed or fallen asleep. They sometimes found him in very obscure places. Usually during these periods, Ajabapa was violent to his young sons; to an extent they must have just absorbed this as a way of being - to manage their father and their lives. They must have engaged in a fair bit of wheeling and dealing to survive their early childhood.

When I spoke to my brother Suresh about his recollections of our Ajabapa and our mamas, he remembers violence, especially against Manekmama, and bad language and swearing. Suresh said it had a profound impact on him and even growing up he hated friends who would resort to swearing, using bad language and treating women badly. He could recall going with our mamas to get alcohol from places for Ajabapa. Gujarat State had prohibition (and still does) so alcohol was purchased on the illegal market. It was because of those early experiences that later my Mum valued my Dad for not drinking much at all.

I recall that in England, Dad poured out brandy like medicine when the bottle would come out of the cupboard, usually when guests came. But it was only the men who were offered any alcohol at a meal. The drink was measured out carefully and put away. When it came to the end of the bottle my Dad would try to squeeze out every drop. Eventually as the stopper had a cork and would seal well, they would wash out the bottle, dry it and use it to store mukhwas (a combination of fennel seeds, betel nuts, and bits which we eat after meal to refresh the mouth). I remember one of the bottles was the Dimple brand, which was an interesting shape and looked enchanting filled with the mukhwas. It was wonderful sight for a young child especially if it had little sugar-coated fennel seeds in assorted colours interspersed. I used to be fascinated when we went for a meal at relatives and friends in England when they produced their own versions of whisky and brandy bottles filled with these beautiful, sugar-coated jewels.

My Mum, being the eldest and a daughter, was the one who saw all aspects of these earlier years and was a real support to Ajima, not just in helping with housework, looking after her siblings, but earning money by cleaning - young girls would go to people's houses to wash dishes. Many still do in rural and city locations where families are just extremely poor. Mum really stopped going to school after she was eight or nine years old to help at home. She also found other ways to help economically by, for instance, collecting chaan (cowpat), drying it and ready for burning. Although I am recounting experiences from over eighty years ago, many poor people still do this to this day even as India is now one of the 'superpowers' on the world stage. I can clearly remember as a young child people collecting chaan, including my Mum in Munsad.

I asked Mum about her experience of collecting it as young child. She recalls that she used to get up at dawn with a friend and usually walk a couple of miles or more to the Muslim area where they kept cows for milking. The cows would leave huge cowpats, and Mum and her friend would look after each other whilst collecting it and walking long distances. They would scoop up the cowpat in baskets. Sometimes the chaan would be runnier and harder to scoop up than when it had the chance to dry and solidify, but they wanted to get it before others did. The baskets were old and with holes so the cowpat would run down at the sides of their heads. They would take as much as possible, and the basket would get very heavy. On one occasion she hurt her back carrying the weight all that distance. She recalls one poor girl whose friend put more chaan in after the basket was loaded onto her head, and a loose bit of the basket shard poked her eye and blinded her. There must be so many stories like that - it is hard to believe. They would also try to collect horse-dung when there were horses and carts around. Often though this would get squashed by vehicles and bicycles, but they would still try to scrape it off the road and collect it anyway. People did have accidents, as there were cars around, and children got injured collecting. Mum recalls that the best was when the circus came to town and most children would be excited to see the acts, but she and her friends were excited by the huge elephant dung which would double their normal 'takings'.

They took it back to their homes and then mixed it with anything that would burn, such as small bits of hay. Sometimes they would try to buy the dregs of coal dust to mix in and make it burn better. It was made into round cakes, dried and used for burning as fuel for cooking.

An interesting anecdote about Munsad that Mum shared, was that in some areas they were not allowed to collect dung as it was contracted for collection by people of the Dalit caste – in effect providing work for extremely poor people in the lowest Hindu caste hierarchy. The Indian Government gave a directive for this as at a basic level it was to address inequality. The Dalit people would collect chaan and put it on the central fields to provide manure and compost heaps that would be spread over the land. The landowners were the contractors. But other people who also needed the cowpat used to collect in areas where it was less strict. After her marriage Mum used to go out collecting with my Dewalima (a widowed aunt from my Dad's side of the family) who was very much in our lives, and they would share the proceeds.

She often told us the story of how my brother Chandra came with her one school lunchtime and helped her, as he did not like my Mum sharing half the proceeds and he was keen for us to have it all for our fuel. It is true my aunt did have a habit of forcing herself on us, but who can blame her as she had four sons and life was hard for widows. To her credit, her sons later went on to own properties and some land in our village, and by any standards were considered very wealthy even before three out of her four sons migrated to America. Dewalima's grandson stayed in Munsad and had real skills with farm machines and working on the land. He did well without taking the route of studying for a degree and/or migrating to succeed. He has land and workers and in all respects is a landowner and a prosperous farmer in Munsad. Some of the property came his way through managing the homes of people who had migrated, and when the older relatives died, he was able to manage the property and eventually bought them from their relatives – many who were living abroad and not likely to come back to live in Munsad. His parents are still in the village, but his uncles and their families have all gone off to America. It is a success story because they really did have nothing but were resilient enough to make it in their place of birth in the village. Dewalima was a notable example of a single widowed woman who withstood adversity, including misogyny and hardship from poverty. She brought up her four sons alone and they had a tough life. They eventually helped to raise her out of poverty and her later years were comfortable. Her family are part of my Dad's kutumb so part of the Munsad family. She came to England in 1985-86 and stayed in my house in Bristol for a few days. This was just after I had been to India in 1984 to visit for the first time after our migration, so I had recently seen her. She was very funny and said she was very proud of me because as a young woman I had bought my first house on my own and without a husband. Although she was proud, she still wanted me to get married and have a husband – an enduring cry from all my relatives throughout my teens, twenties, and early thirties.

This brings me to the rest of my Dad's side of the family from the village of Munsad.

Munsad family

My paternal grandfather (who we refer to as 'Bapa') was Makanbhai, and his father was Kalan Lallabhai. I do not know much about this side of the family except that my Bapa, Makan Kalan (son of Kalan so known as Makan Kalan) went abroad from his village to work in South Africa.

Recent research and analysis of slavery and colonial history sheds light on how our grandparents' generation ended up in places like South Africa and East Africa. After slavery was abolished in 1807 in the UK, the British needed labour in their developing colonies and many Indian men were recruited to work as indentured workers. The villagers were often illiterate, and they would sign a contract to agree to work abroad. It is possible that once the men could see others going, they would feel a degree of reassurance to be with group of others from their village. That is how my paternal grandfather Makanbapa ended up in South Africa as a labourer for a period.

My family on both sides seem to have been migrating abroad to earn money even in the late 1800s and early 1900s. One of the photographs I have is my Bapa in a photo of his Bhajan Mandal group.

Bhajan Mandal group taken in South Africa. Makanbapa is on the far left, top row.

This is a bit like an Indian version of a gospel group, as they were religious choirs. It is on the one hand a wonderful image of rural Indian men, dressed in their best worn and frayed Victorian outfits reserved for official occasions; but is also an image of men so far away from their home, working hard as labourers. I rescued this framed faded photograph on my first visit to our Munsad home in 1984 trip and it conveys so much to me about my Bapa's short life.

On my Makanbapa's side there was no obvious landownership or inheritance of property and many, including his brother Icchabhai, went abroad. In caste terms, we Prajapatis were overall a choti jat in that we were lower caste and were not landowners. Hence men in our families went abroad almost certainly as unskilled labourers. Mum says she heard stories about 'the plague' and 'Spanish flu' around 1918 and 1919 that spurred people from communities like ours to migrate to countries that offered economic incentives to work. Interestingly it was not to settle abroad but just to earn money, as they were generally uneducated and had no skills for careers. Permanent migration came later for those who stayed, settled and became firmly part of the East African Asian diaspora

Makanbapa　　　　　　　　　　　　*Laduma*

My Makanbapa was born in 1895 and died on 29 December 1937 aged forty-two. My paternal grandmother Laduben was born on 31 May 1895 and died six months before Dad died, so she was over seventy.

There are not many stories about Makanbapa as he was away some of the time and died when my Dad was only fifteen (the same as I was when my Dad died). Bapa and Laduma had six children - two daughters and four sons. They were Jiviben, Parbhubhai, Lalbhai (known as Chagan), Bennaben, Naranbhai and the youngest my Dad, Dahyabhai.

Jiviben, our phoi (aunt), I do remember well. She was married off to a man with whom she could not have children. She was beaten often because of 'being barren' and eventually a divorce was decreed by a gathering of five men from the family or community known as panchayat. She was then married off to a man who had previously been married and widowed three times and had two children, so she became a stepmother to Dhanjibhai and Lalbhai who later became significant in our lives. I remember Dhanjibhai very well as a young child growing up in Leicester. In the early and late 1960's he was instrumental in helping people of our community to get jobs and had a link into various industries. In a way he was an early 'community worker' and involved in getting our Prajapati presence established in Leicester. His brother Lalbhai was a tailor and he and my Dad went back to Kenya to set up a tailor's shop while we were in India. I will explore that later as the story unfolds.

Jiviphoi had a son, but it was a difficult birth, and he died during the delivery. So she was not 'barren', but maybe her first husband had been the one with the problem of conception. To me she was the first significant role model of a strong woman, even though she was not independent in a modern feminist sense. She was someone who could speak her mind and was described as a hard worker. She used to visit us and I remember her as a larger-than-life personality. I have fond memories of her bringing us little gifts of foodstuffs and she was a refreshing change from her mother, my Laduma, who was a more introverted and a sad figure. Jiviphoi seemed fun, a real character, endearing and inspiring.

Jiviphoi was resilient and independent but, like so many people who supported their children to migrate, she was left to fend for herself and died a lonely death. Many women who survived their husbands and whose family had migrated, lived and died without close family members near them, making something of a mockery of the stereotype of 'Asians looking after their own families'. Mum tells me my Dad would have sent us both back to India to look after our Laduma and her daughter-in-law (our Bhulima), but he had a stroke before he could arrange this. For our immediate family in India and England, it was just a matter of survival and improving our life as best we could.

As Mum gets older, she does reflect on the life of her mother-in-law and my Bhulima. My Mum had a tough early life, but she feels luckier than the women in our family in India who died without immediate relatives around them. The lives of the people left behind are often sad stories that are very painful to discuss. We got the chance to migrate and to become (to varying degrees) economically 'successful' at the cost of leaving our grandparents and aunts behind. It is the great untold story of the sacrifice made by those left behind during migration. We tend to focus on the struggles of migration, racism and the difficulties we encountered and not on the people left behind. It is now only my generation who came over as young children who have a memory of living in India who can make that connection with the people they left behind. Our children will not have that similar connection.

Parbhubhai and Chaganbhai, the two brothers (known to us as Bapas) married two sisters Bhuliben and Naniben (known to us as Mas). Bhulima and Parbhubapa lived in Ahmedabad because of his employment as a carpenter. However, they were one of the first to go to Kenya on a sailing boat (varan), which was a basic way to travel and extremely dangerous. Bhulima had two beautiful sons delivered by caesarean section all those years ago. She was advised not to have any more children due to difficulties she might have in subsequent pregnancies. Consequently she was sterilised. It is not clear what the issue was but appeared to have been serious so could have been something like pre-eclampsia. Unfortunately, and tragically for them their sons both died from smallpox and so they then became 'childless'. Chaganbapa was supported to go to Kenya with Nanima by Ichhabapa (their uncle, Kaka), so the two brothers and the two sisters lived in Nairobi at that time.

Although Parbhubapa was an attentive and kind husband according to my Mum's recollection, people rated his brother, our Chaganbapa, as brighter and more intelligent. Parbhubapa was a bit of a drinker. Mum said he would drink a bottle of whisky for a bet. In any case there was a family argument between the brothers and so Parbhubapa and Bhulima went off to Mombasa. At the same time Mum and Dad were getting married in India. By the time my Mum was to join my Dad in Nairobi, Parubapa had died and Bhulima's life had changed dramatically, becoming a widow with no income and no children of her own. Once Mum got to Nairobi, Bhulima came back to Munsad as a widow to live in the family home and care for her sasu (our Laduma) just 3 months after her husband died, and she never left the village. She lost everything at an early age.

As children, my brothers and I were close to Bhulima as she had a kind nature. When we were growing up most adults in our village seemed 'rough and ready', but Bhulima was one of the nurturing people who was an important part of our lives. I was particularly close to her as my Mum often used to go off to Navsari when we lived in India. I would wait around for Mum's last bus and get terribly upset if she did not come home. It meant sleeping with my Laduma. I hated sleeping with Laduma as she smelled of snuff and had a bed made from coarse ropes called kathia. In India we did not have the luxury of a mattress. I would prefer to sleep with my Bhulima as she was our mother substitute when our own Mum was not around. Also, her bed was made from patta – a sort of interlaced elastic, which was not as harsh as Laduma's.

Naranbapa was described as 'a hard nut'; he threatened his mother Laduma and got into a lot of debt after moving to Bombay. He had a wife, but she died in childbirth. He remarried and had a baby daughter called Bhiki who also died at the age of three. His wife had gone to help a family member with childbirth and had a heart attack and died whilst assisting. Consequently, Naranbapa lived a sad life and had ill health. Bhulima did help look after Naranbapa after he was widowed and lost his children and Chaganbapa paid off his debts. It was a sad life for those relatives.

My Dad was born on 18 September 1922. He went to school, then started a tailoring course (apprenticed to tailors doing all sorts of jobs). It was not until he was twenty-one that he went to Kenya after discussing his future with his brother Chaganbhai. At that age he would normally be married but he deferred this, trying to find a way of learning a skill. It is not clear why he waited so long to migrate but when he did, he went to Nairobi and entered what seems to have been another apprenticeship.

Dad taken at a studio in his early 20's

He told my Mum that they made him do all sorts of work, but he was with a good firm and learnt his trade observing skilled tailors. It gave him immense pride that he became a skilled gents' tailor. Gujarati men also did women's tailoring, making blouses and petticoats for wearing under saris. My Dad felt this was not as skilled a job as making shirts and suits. Those years, for Dad before his marriage, consisted of working, paying rent and food costs, reimbursing his brother for any financial help he may have given such as the fare for his passage to Kenya from India, then saving to go back to India and pay for the wedding, or at least his contribution, as some would come from the bridal side. My Dad was quite principled, and Mum has often said he was not the kind even in those days to exploit the dowry system. As with most men working abroad, he would send money home for his mother to run the home, but I suspect it was not a huge amount as not much was left from the meagre salary of an apprentice. Our early days in England later made me realise how frugally we all lived to stretch the money and to save a tiny amount to send to our family back home. It is also how migrants from poor countries who come to England nowadays manage too. All live hand to mouth and there is no room for non-essentials of any description.

Dad initially stayed in Kenya for five years and saved enough money to return to India to get married. His plan was to stay for four weeks to find a bride, get married and return to Nairobi to pick up work. He took a bit longer: it was to be three months before he went back to Nairobi after the wedding in May 1948. Mum followed to join him around November 1949.

Mum was only fifteen and my Dad was twenty-six when they married. My Mum had grown up in a city whilst Dad had lived in a rural village only a few miles away, but which was vastly different. Dad was an older, severe man but Mum had not even started menstruating at the time of her marriage. My Ajima kept this fact from my Dad as she did not want to jeopardise her daughter's chance of the opportunity of a good marriage with a foreign-based suitor. From my Ajima's point of view and in the context of the times it made sense. Her daughter Laxmi would hopefully have a better life materially and going abroad was (and still is) considered to offer better opportunities and a better future. The fact that Mum was just a girl and my Dad a man of twenty-six was not such a taboo at the time, but my Dad was under the impression that Mum had started her menstrual cycle. However, Mum tells me that she only started to menstruate soon after the wedding. It averted what would have been a difficult scenario, both for my Mum and Dad and for Ajima who might have been seen to have lied - something my Dad would have held against her.

Dad was alerted to this young girl as a prospective bride by a family relative and Ajima was keen on the match immediately, despite the age difference. The opportunity for her daughter to marry someone living abroad was of prime importance given that her own set up was very precarious with an alcoholic husband and hungry mouths to feed. Marrying off daughters is a major preoccupation for any Indian family, but at that time, it was particularly hard. Mum tells me there was a bit of a controversy about the fact she was from Navsari as there had been two other women who had married into Dad's extended family, both from Navsari. These unions had both ended in divorce, so there was a feeling amongst Dad's family that Navsari girls were not suited for village life. Dad was the kind to make up his own mind and trusted the relative who was the intermediary, so the wedding went ahead.

Their wedding took place in midst of rationing and there were restrictions on the wedding party and on food. Predictably money was tight, and her Bhikhimasi in South Africa sent Mum the wedding sari. Sadly, the sari did not arrive early enough, and when it did it was not lovely silk or chiffon but lugudu which was pink cotton voile. It is still not clear why she was sent a lugudu as even in those days it was not the most fashionable of fabrics. Ajima had it embroidered to make it look more festive as a wedding sari. Dad was supposed to bring a sari from his family for Mum to change into to travel to her new home, to show symbolically that she now belonged to them. It was, and still is, the custom but Dad did not bring one and Mum missed out yet again. There was a wedding party, food, and an effort was made to keep my Ajabapa from becoming drunk and to keep a semblance of order and respectability.

Mum and Dad after their wedding

It must have all been so difficult leaving aside the fact that Mum's life to that date had been one of looking after her parents and siblings. Her own needs were subsumed by her worry about the family she was leaving. Dad, in common with the men of his family and generation, was chauvinistic and a typical patriarch. There was also an old-fashioned view that the city girls were soft, and rural girls were hardy, and she was subjected to various tests to prove her worth. One was to lift a slab of rock on which clothes were usually washed. She was made to carry that slab on her back for some distance. This slab must have weighed as much as her little frame which was only six and a half stone - if that. Mum was at that age very thin and wiry like other young girls brought up in poor families in the India of the 1940's. She says she remembers the weight and her legs bending to the pressure. It seems archaic - it was and still is! I have no doubt this practice still goes on in places all over the world where women are living in almost feudal communities. There is no other way of explaining it, other than men in villages playing silly games. She also had to a carry a big bag containing a fine substance like cement on her head, up the stairs to the decrepit loft area in our old house. The prejudice about a 'soft city girl' was compounded by the two divorces of Navsari women in our kutumb (extended family). So, there was a view that city girls could not cope with rural life and work in the fields – hence the macabre tests. Somehow my Mum withstood all this humiliation and in time she more than proved her worth and has outlived them all.

Dad went back to Kenya within three months of arriving back in India, having married and being keen to start earning again. During that period Mum was still a new wife and living a short bus ride from her parents' family in Navsari. She had to acclimatise to rural village life, working in the fields and being a new member of the household. The traditional hierarchy would be the total authority of the sasu (mother-in-law), then the other women who were there before her would be senior in status. This was not so much the case in our family as my Laduma was not that type of woman. She was an introverted, quiet figure who would be incapable of exercising authority and control over anyone. To some extent we do not know if that was her nature, or if she experienced difficulties which we were not aware of. She was not a stereotypical Indian sasu who exercised her powers over her wovs (daughters-in-law). She was opposite to the caricature of a dominating Indian sasu. There were no immediate male figures in our household, but Icchabapa was the 'elder statesman' of our extended family, the kutumbi, and my Dad's uncle. He would keep all the women in the extended family a bit under his grip as the other men in my family who were still alive were living abroad. The patriarchy and authority of men seem to permeate even from one man.

My Mum continued to support her own mother (my Ajima) as best she could. It was good she had time to grow and develop before going to Kenya to join Dad. These eighteen months helped her to settle into a different life, before the demands of marital life in a foreign country. Also, learning how to live with my Laduma and Bhulima in a rural village was an important transition phase. As described earlier Bhulima had been recently widowed and had come back from Africa and was dependent on family support. My Mum said that since she was not familiar with working in the fields, she was nervous about the possible dangers but could not show her fear. Laduma had rented a little kyando (small plot of land) from the local Parsi landowners but because she was not able to pay adequate rent on it, she was allocated the bit at the bottom end of a slope which would get flooded and there were a lot of roots from trees and shrubs that made growing very difficult. But Mum would go out with Laduma and try to help. She admits she hated it and preferred to cook, which suited Bhulima who hated cooking, so they may have led a peaceful life carving out roles which allowed coexistence without the rivalry that is common in extended households.

Power and status were just as important in the matriarchal hierarchy as in the patriarchal one. Fortunately, Laduma was not combative, and neither was she controlling or seeking to enforce her power over her daughters-in-law. Mum has said she was lucky in that Laduma was not like that and although she feared living in rural village Laduma and Bhulima made her life easier. When they went to their little bit of the field, she would step in Laduma's footsteps so she would not step on a scorpion, snakes, or deadly insects. Their footwear, if they existed, would be flip flops, but at that time they were likely to be barefoot. Years of working and living barefoot had hardened the soles of their feet but they still were very vulnerable to bites and injuries from thorns. People did hurt themselves and died from bites and infections, which increased Mum's fear. Laduma kept a couple of cows, but it is not clear if she got much milk out of them as grass and feed was scarce. In all our family talks about Laduma, everyone says she was remarkably close to her animals and cared for and nurtured them in a way she could not with people.

As described earlier, the Prajapati caste are skilled artisans and crafts people, and my family were potters (Kumbhars) by trade. Laduma made choolah – something like a raised almost circular firepit on which you would balance pots, and under which one built a fire, so it was possible to cook on it. They were cooking structures made from clay. Amazingly choolah came up as a word on a TV programme I used to watch as a young woman, called 'Call my Bluff.' Although a trivial fact it got me excited as I wondered who had set the question. An Indian researcher from my caste? There were not any of us around in those days behind the scenes on television, so it stayed in my mind as a memorable occasion, and of course I knew the answer!

Laduma also made katchi bheet, which translates as unfired bricks, and the middle of our house was held up by these precarious bricks. I suspect that since they were unfired, they would disintegrate and need replacing over time. Another thing that Laduma made was a granary store known as kothi made from mud, mixed with straw, and hardened. Grains would be poured into the top opening, then it was sealed at the bottom opening, allowing grain to be taken out as needed and closed off in between use. Making that would be quite a skilful job especially as she was quite small in stature. There was also a smaller, more refined dafoda with a smaller funnel and involved even greater skill. As well as that she made matli, which were thinner earthenware pots for storing water after collection from the wells. It was only in discussing this with my Mum, that I really began to understand how skilful Laduma was as a potter. I do not think I have ever heard anyone praise her work in my family.

By the time Mum was preparing to join Dad in Kenya, Ajima was pregnant with my Ramilamasi, so it was hard for Mum to leave her as she was still the one supporting Ajima with practical help. Mum and Ajima were more like sisters than mother and daughter and Ajima must have felt her loss acutely. I cannot imagine the emotional scenes between Mum and

Ajima when Mum finally left India. I witnessed many emotional scenes between them over the years so can only assume it was an immense wrench.

Going off to Kenya to join my Dad must have been devastating for this young girl just turning seventeen. She had not travelled much outside her town and my Dad's village, other than in the general district of Surat where our relatives lived. Her world had been so narrow and contained but now she was going on a steam ship to Africa – another continent – without knowing what was in store. The journey would have been long and arduous. She told me it was about ten days but could not remember the details. Her own limited education must have made her feel so isolated as lack of knowledge is disempowering and her confidence like a lot of women of little experience must have been a notch below zero. It must have been an extraordinary journey for a young Indian woman from a poor family who had a very scarce contact with people outside her immediate family structure. One consolation is that at that time other people from our area were making similar trips, so she was not travelling entirely on her own. Mum recalls that there were three other people making that journey with her from near Navsari. She travelled to Mombasa on the boat before getting a train to Nairobi, so it must have been a formidable trip. Her knowledge of Swahili or English was non-existent and added to her isolation once on Kenyan soil.

This was more of a start of a proper married life with my Dad. However, she was without her extended family nearby and she was living in a foreign country colonised by the British. She had had a transition phase whilst living in Munsad without Dad and all the marital demands that would have entailed, getting used to a life outside Navsari and becoming a new wov (daughter-in-law). Up to that point she had traversed childhood into womanhood, from a person who only knew her village and city to travelling to another unknown continent. I often wonder what Mum thought as she left her family this first time to go to Africa. Did she know she may return or was it just putting her fate in in 'God's Hand'? So many people did who had faith but limited education or control of their life.

She would return to Mother India in 1957 with three children and her husband after seven years in Africa. She never referred to Kenya as her home and we were not part of the East African Asian diaspora who would go on to be expelled as part of the Africanisation policy post-independence of East African countries.

Kenya years

These few years in Nairobi were difficult and challenging for her as she had to come to terms with being an incredibly young wife and a mother to her son within a brief time of arriving. By the end of 1955 she had become a mother to three children. It was also a struggle to live well in Kenya, since they were not educated enough to capitalise on the fruits of colonialism which benefitted some Indians who went to live there. They were an important part of the workforce for the British, and the Asians were used to 'divide and rule' with the Kenyan people. This 'divide and rule' philosophy enabled some Asians to see themselves as 'above' the Kenyan people in the hierarchy of career and status. The Indian population, if educated to a certain level (modern GCSE level), became a new middle class and functioned as a buffer between the African people and the British colonial masters. Dad's education was more limited, and he did not have the basics to work in the type of government jobs which were available to Indians who had passed their matriculation exams in India or abroad. The ones with these basic qualifications got administrative jobs which gave them good salaries and pensions. Dad was literate but as a tailor would always be on 'piecework' – effectively paid minimum wages for work done, and that would be low paid in any country. He never had a pension attached to any of his jobs. I am so proud that my parents were not in a class that would or could have exploited the people of Kenya.

Mum's account is that they had a very tough time, living in poor conditions in respect of accommodation and living on a single wage. She gave birth to my eldest brother, just before her eighteenth birthday in 1951. He was a small baby and was most probably over protected by a young mother who had little support. Although they had my aunt and uncle nearby (Chaganbapa and Nanima), my Mum was quite isolated, and my Dad was strict and controlling so she did not have friends. Mum often does not have historical or political perspectives to contextualise her experiences, but she does recall Princess Elizabeth coming to Kenya as a 25-year-old with her new husband in the same year my brother Suresh was born. Early in February 1952 the Princess found out about her father's death, and that she would be crowned Queen Elizabeth II. My Mum, like many South Asians of her age were very fond of the Queen.

At the time of writing the Queen has died at the age of ninety-six. She had a big state funeral on Monday 19th September 2022, and Mum alongside many people watched the TV all day. The British do 'pomp and circumstance' very well and Elizabeth II's long reign would pull at the strings of that generation of the colonial subjects of the old Commonwealth. When the Queen died there was a powerful sense by our government that her funeral should be a one of the biggest occasions in history. People recognised that Britain was stamping its authority as a player on the world stage, possibly for the very last time, in a world that sees Britain as more peripheral in its dominance than before.

Back in Kenya, my second brother came along quite soon and Mum has recently spoken about how she considered having an abortion. However, by the time she realised she was expecting, her pregnancy was well advanced, and the doctor warned her against any intervention. When she got home from the doctor's appointment, she said she wept. But Dad said they would get through this difficult patch with God's help, and thankfully she gave birth to a healthy son. Chandra was born seventeen months after Suresh, arriving in April 1953.

She talks about an incident when a minor dispute with her older Indian neighbours over milk escalated to her being ostracised by them. They taunted her on having another baby in quick succession and whilst pregnant with Chandra they would lock the communal bathroom and deprive her of using the toilet and facilities for washing clothes. Obviously, washing was all done by hand from a running tap, and it seems appalling that they would behave like that towards a woman with a baby and expecting a second. Suresh did not have the freedom of other toddlers due to the bullying by the neighbours. It is one of the recurring themes she talks about that as the eldest child being brought up in this situation meant he was subject to far more restrictions. She toilet trained him early and moved to bottle feeds earlier than she wanted to so she could breast feed Chandra without causing problems for Suresh.

In those days in Kenya, women were hospitalised in the maternity hospital for ten days after the birth. Dad would take Suresh to my aunt and uncle in the morning, go to work and then pick him up after teatime. Then Dad would take him to hospital to see Mum and his new baby brother. Mum says she was so distressed to be away from home and Suresh that she begged to go home earlier, and she got home after 8 days. The situation with the neighbours continued to be difficult and it prevented her from having close friends in Kenya as their behaviour was so vindictive and disproportionate. It helped reinforce my Dad's view not to get too involved with others. She had two miscarriages before having me (only two and half years later) and she acknowledges that she may have helped the miscarriages along - in a similar way to what she had observed others do, including her own mother, taking dubious concoctions to bring on miscarriages. Successive and often unwanted pregnancies were common with her peer group. She was clear in her mind that she could not face another child so soon after Chandra and is able to talk about it more freely and openly to me and now more openly to other family members in her nineties; a frightening experience to go through on your own without good friends and families nearby. The lack of proper contraception and control over women's bodies meant that people had more children than they wanted. Many of our relatives had four to six children but our family and my Chaganbapa's family were exceptions to the rule with just Balwantbhai and Bhaniben, our cousins. Hearing Mum's story makes one realise how women took risks to terminate their pregnancies to provide a reasonable life for the ones who were born and to protect their physical and mental health. This is a perennial debate about women's right to choose and have control, but things seem even worse in the modern age of contraception with religious zealotry which in the USA has just recently (2023) overturned a famous victory (Roe v. Wade) and 'Women's Right to Choose'. It is possible that many women of Mum's generation of migrants suffered terrible undiagnosed mental health problems when there was little vocabulary, let alone understanding, about the consequences of unwanted pregnancies and post-natal depression. Conversely, infertility of any description often scarred a married woman's life, and some women were divorced by their husbands, even when it was the male who may have been infertile – as was the case for my Jiviphoi.

During the Kenya years, the main form of communication was letter writing via a paper-thin blue airmail or sending a letter back with people who were going home. The 'air letter' was posted by airmail and was a thin sheet folded for writing inside with the ends sealed for the address of sender and the recipient on the outside. This thin blue sheet carried the news there and back from home and abroad and conveyed all the moments of loss, love, joy, and news of celebrations, sadness and happiness. The handwriting was compressed, and all available space was used around the edges. I have seen many letters over the years and wish I had photographed one of my Ajima's to share how carefully they were written to convey maximum news using minimum space. Alas, most have been shredded as I helped Mum go through her collection. I know their significance from our time in India and England. There would have been moments of waiting, then receiving the letter through the letterbox, putting it away, opening it up, and savouring the news alone when the family were asleep or busy. I remember her subdued sobs as she read news from Desh. Despite Mum's limited education she could read and write and says both improved when Suresh and Chandra started school in India.

A selection of airmail letters

Mum would have waited eagerly to get my Ajima's letters with the news about how the family were managing. Amazingly, Ajima also had enough reading and writing skills to value this form of communication. She would write an account of my Ajabapa's ventures into new projects. Some of these projects were funded by Bhikhima (Ajima's sister) and her husband in South Africa - they continued to be incredibly supportive to Ajima and helped set Ajabapa up with a business selling crockery and in carpentry related ventures. This was due to loyalty for Ajima and wanting to help Ajabapa to find a gainful employment to ward off the drinking and help him provide for the family. Ajima also sent news to my Dad about Laduma and Bhulima from Munsad and there was a sense that people were looking out for each other in those early years. The family members were still relatively young then and able to travel and support each other in those days after we migrated.

In Nairobi my family initially lived in a rented room, but they were subsequently given notice to leave as the houses the tenants occupied were earmarked for demolition. Mum was pregnant with me, and they eventually found a room in another house. It was a room usually reserved for a 'boy' – often a term for a servant who worked and did chores in the main house. The term is undoubtedly a remnant from the days of slavery. It was a basic room in which we lived, cooked, and slept. In this confined room my Mum looked after three children under four. Suresh was asthmatic and I developed a growth behind my right ear which got exceptionally large and infected. According to Mum, my brothers would tell her if my wound was weeping and keep a watchful eye, swatting off flies from the wound. Mum would not agree to have it operated on and after an ordeal I recovered without any surgery. Amazingly I did not die of infection. I still have a scar behind my right ear. Years later in my fifties, I went on to get a serious benign brain tumour leading to a facial palsy and loss of total hearing in my left ear following the diagnosis and treatment of facial nerve neuroma. It was unconnected to my childhood illness, but the problem with my other ear, was to dominate health issues in my later years and to this day.

Dad was out at work during the day. At weekends, they would visit Chaganbapa and Nanima and their children Bhaniben and Balwantbhai but the rest of the time Mum coped on her own. She learnt to embroider, and apart from cooking and cleaning and looking after us, she managed to snatch moments of creativity with her embroidery. Dad gave Mum decent quality white suit cloths and printed patterns for her to decorate. She embroidered sheets and throws and pillowcases and crocheted borders to hang off the edge of the pillowcases. She was very skilled, and these sheets and pillowcases have come with us all the way here to England. Larger sheets were worn out with use and discarded, but I have inherited her pillowcases as they were often used to adorn the beds so have stayed in good condition. It is amazing to think she would have had time to do this, but it is also a sign of the very insular life she lived.

In her late eighties, I reintroduced her to embroidery and she has worked on napkins, pillowcases and tablecloths. Now in her nineties, she has given up much of this but until very recently was still enjoying growing spinach, coriander and garlic in the garden. She says one of the reasons she was able to do so much embroidery in Kenya was because we were very well-behaved children. We had no toys to speak of and would play with empty cotton bobbins from Dad's sewing threads. Once she tried to get a blow-up elephant as they were cheap, but Chandra was frightened by the toy, so she took it back. The combination of a strict father and a lack of real choice made us compliant as infants and toddlers.

It is quite remarkable how Mum coped in a strange land - it feels as if Mum's life lacked any sense of community and friendships. Later we would see these relatives again in Leicester, England with their expanding families. Chaganbapa, Nanima, Balwantbhai, Bhaniben and the children that followed all lived near us and we did have a very active involvement and fond relationship with each other. We still do over half a century later.

It was a hard life for people like my parents and particularly Mum as they were on the lower rung in a country where the Kenyan people themselves were exploited under colonialism. Asians whose families had moved to Kenya as descendants of earlier indentured servants and labourers for the British and had stayed, or who came as a more educated cohort, got good jobs and were becoming established and settled. They began to have businesses and property, and to accumulate some wealth, so their children were getting a decent education. We, on the other hand, were poor migrant villagers and living just above or below the basic living standard of the Kenyans, Ugandans, or the other people of the African colonies. Later in the 1970's, most Asian people were expelled from Uganda by Idi Amin's regime as part of his 'Africanisation' policy. 'Asians' as a term encompassed all the people who had migrated from the Indian subcontinent and were all viewed by Amin and other African leaders as a part of the colonial exploitation of their land and businesses.

I do not have any memories of Nairobi or Kenya as I was only eighteen months old when we went back to India. My brothers were five and three. Interestingly, in England now if you say you were born in Kenya, we get associated with people known as 'Kenyan or Ugandan Asians'. I often meet Kenyan Asians who talk with such nostalgia for Africa; for them I could see they lost their homes and a good life. Ours was nothing like what they left behind. Therefore, it is difficult to compare different waves of Asian migration and their experiences, especially in Britain. Many people make vast generalisations, but there are some real differences in our experiences in settling in Britain.

Meanwhile, Dad had lost his job in Nairobi, as the business employing him was making a loss and they said they had no choice but to lay him off. I found one of those letters in his bag of papers; envisioning him getting that letter is so heart breaking. This happened a couple of times over the years, and he had to take stock of what he did next with this growing family and no wages. He and his sibling were still supporting their mother and sister-in-law in India. My parents decided to go back to India to be with our relatives in Munsad to plan what they did next.

Family return to India

We went back to India and our village in the summer of 1957 travelling by boat to stay with my paternal grandmother Laduma and my aunt Bhulima.

Dad got to work to sort out the creaking family house, which was dilapidated, unsafe and needing urgent repair. Our widowed aunt, Bhulima had no living children and Chaganbapa, Nanima and their children were still in Kenya. It was likely that they were going to stay in Kenya for a while. The house in India was a family home that belonged to Dad and all his brothers and their offspring. During the following nine months he was with us, he set to work to get the house repaired and make plans for our next move as he was running out of money and had to think about our future. He was encouraged to go back to Kenya with his step-nephew Lalbhai (Jiviphoi's stepson), who was also a tailor.

Lalbhai's wife had recently taken her own life by throwing herself into a well. It seems shocking but over my childhood I often heard about drastic ways in which women took their lives including setting fire to themselves. Not as a sati, where women would take their own lives after becoming a widow as an act of devotion - but in dire circumstances when women resorted to ultimate self-harm and taking their own lives. Whether it was depression or repression which led to such act of ultimate self-harm is hard to say but growing up I heard that it was just 'one of those things.' The fact that it happened to women was not often questioned.

Later in Coventry, England, my Mum's cousin (Pushpamasi) a mother of three boys, set herself alight in the bathroom and died in the late 1960's. We used to spend time with her sister Shantimasi and her children. Pushpamasi and her family lived in the same street as her sister, so we saw them on our visits. I was a young child, and her death had a profound effect on me. I had really liked her. Even as a child I sensed she was unhappy, and I did not like her husband who seemed indifferent to her sadness. It is likely she was very depressed, and he did not know how to support her. It is also likely she had undiagnosed post-natal depression after her sons were born. Many men of that generation, and even the current generation, struggle with how to support their partners through mental health crises arising from childbirth. In addition, services catering for different ethnicities were not around at all in those days. Hopefully, cities like Coventry and Leicester would have better signposts and services now. Even so, the whole policy, planning and provision of mental health across the country, including for different ages, ethnicities, gender and LGBTQ+ people is sadly very patchy and variable across Britain. Her sons were much younger than us when she took her own life. It is unimaginable what the impact of losing their mother will have had on them.

Back in India, Lalbhai and my Dad planned to return to Kenya, pool their resources and open a new tailor's shop in Nairobi. They would stock other things like haberdashery as well as undertaking commission for suits, shirts and Lalbhai would do the women's tailoring. Without the family drain on either of their time they could work long hours and make money. They could live in cheap lodgings and just make a go of it without the family for two or three years, sending money back to support them but saving as much as possible. It seemed like a good plan, and they went off back to Kenya in the spring of 1958, leaving us in Munsad.

Photo sent to my Dad in Kenya. Chandra, Tara and Suresh

Our family are not great entrepreneurs, but also due to the state of the economy, within two years of the shop opening it closed, and the stock was sold off. I always thought Dad had gone straight to England after we returned to India but this period of him trying to run a business was news to me while researching for this book. It reminded me of my eldest brother Suresh trying to set up a TV repair shop in Leicester in the late 1980's. It was very distressing to see him attempt to get it going and sinking his savings into it, only for him to eventually close it and work for wages again. I believe our family are best serving people either in the public or the private sector – we do not seem to possess the ruthlessness or business acumen needed. I know it is possible to be ethical and a businessperson, but we did not have the business mentality. We certainly had no appetite for exploiting anyone. We were here to serve our community or the wider community. Hence Chandra became an NHS doctor, and I worked as a professional social worker in various roles in the public sector with a strong emphasis on enabling empowerment for marginal voices. Suresh had been strongly involved in helping the local community through his religious faith in the Swadhya movement. He now volunteers his time to various charitable causes including fundraising after he retired from paid work.

Dad in Kenya then England

Meanwhile in Kenya, Dad was not sure of his next steps but Lalbhai's brother was in England and encouraged his brother and my Dad (his Mama) to join a growing community in England.

'England needs our labour and where we can build a better future for our families,' said the knowledgeable people who were looking elsewhere after Africa as a possible next destination. The 1948 Nationality Act had granted UK citizenship to the citizens of Britain's colonies and there was a growing and sizeable population of Gujaratis moving to England and sending money back to India for their families. This was always a useful indicator of reasons to leave the familiarity and comfort of the homeland. One of the motivations for migration was that people saw money trickling from England to families back home – a tangible proof that it was worth the struggle to leave Desh, the homeland. This was especially so for families like ours who had no inherited wealth or land.

At first, Dad was not keen to go to England as he was in poor health and the thought of living in a cold country did not appeal. However, he realised that Kenya was not going to offer more to our family in the way of prospects, so he had no option but to make that next step to England. He and Lalbhai headed to England's East Midland town of Leicester. Lalbhai's brother Dhanjibhai (mentioned earlier) was in Leicester and was already something of a community organiser, helping the newly moved Gujarati families into the inner-city Belgrave/Melton Road area. He had forged links with trade unions and employers looking for workers and was able to get men work. Single men tended to move in with other Gujarati men living in overcrowded houses and working in a hostile alien environment with experiences of both racism and harsh weather. Men tended to migrate on their own and send for their families later, as was to happen to us. Many men suffered from tuberculosis (TB) and similar illnesses due to living in overcrowded conditions. Dad had to go to a nursing home when suspected of having TB, although it turned out he just had bronchitis at the time. However, the doctors did pick up a problem with my Dad's heart and he was advised to have surgery to address an issue with his heart valve. Dad would have been very frightened by any surgery on the heart. For people from rural India, heart surgery would have equated to a death sentence and none of the medical staff would have explained that this was a routine type of surgery and in fact may have saved him from the early stroke he suffered. His other worry was to earn money and get us over to England and repay any debts incurred in the process. He often told Mum he did not want us to be left with debts and so any surgery would be perceived as a real risk of leaving the family with financial problems if he did not survive.

Photo sent to Dad in England. Suresh, Tara, Chandra & Mum. Suresh and Chandra and I are wearing clothes made by Dad. The same shorts/shirts feature on many photos and only came out for formal studio photos. We all wore toy watches and apparently Tara's socks have holes you can see but we always thought it was a pattern

Dad and men like him were subject to severe racism at this time and were only able to find rented accommodation in the inner-city area of Belgrave ward in Leicester with Asian landlords. Most people have heard about the signs on doors of rented accommodation stating, 'No coloureds, no Irish and no dogs.' We certainly remember seeing them when we arrived, and we lived amongst these signs which included 'No Wogs' for years. Our parents and their friends had to be resilient and took whatever was on offer, especially as they could not afford to waste money on luxuries. Racism, suspicion of banks and prejudice meant they tended to save enough for an extremely basic house, helping each other pool resources so they could buy properties without mortgages. They would pay back their family and friends rather than face the racist institutions. In time in Leicester, there were people from our community who set up as insurance and mortgage brokers, but this was a bit later.

On reflection, while we were in India without Dad, he was experiencing the harshest period of life in England. He was just working all the time, saving every penny, and experiencing ill health exacerbated by extremely cold winters in overcrowded accommodation with poor facilities and putting up with racism in the workplace while not able to speak the language adequately.

Dad and his friends had little time to gather money to buy houses for their families as clearly the political climate and legislation around commonwealth migration was tightening. The introduction of the Commonwealth Immigrants Act 1962 was a racist intervention to prevent people coming from the colonies who were Black or Asian. It was another incentive for people like my Dad to get us over to this country sooner rather than later. Many of Dad's acquaintances followed suit and sent for their families. It was the fear of being separated as a family longer term and without a choice that made everything more urgent.

Writers like A. Sivanandan (who later wrote the classic, 'A Different Hunger: Writings on Black Resistance') and the sociologist/activist/academic Ruth Glass were important outspoken critics against the racist legislation of the 60's. Kenneth Leech's booklet 'The Birth of a Monster –the growth of racist legislation since 1950s' (based on a paper given at the AGM of the Joint Council for the Welfare of Immigrants) pays homage to Ruth Glass' work and explores how the legislation between 1962-68 is seen as the 'nationalisation of racism'.

The Munsad years

When I talked to Suresh in 2012 about those early years, he told me that arriving in India from Kenya was a blur. He remembered our house being very dark with little sunlight. I was reminded how dark the house was inside when I went back in 1984. The sunlight just came in through the doors, but even in the daytime the house was dark. Inside the house was divided in the middle with storage containers for wheat and rice which my Ma had made as explained earlier.

Inside of our house in Munsad. Janet took three photos and put them together in 1984, so 21 years after we left. The house had been renovated and rented out, so a lot has changed including the grain stores which have gone. The walls are newly painted, but it gives a good impression of where we lived so is included in this Part. Diwalima and my Mum are in the background – the front of the house. You can just see the swing bed near the front door, where most of the light comes in

The house had a front yard in which our cows were tethered and when the rice had been harvested from the fields, it would be stacked there. The long main room was where all the daily activities happened, and grain was stored. I do recall snakes and all sorts of creatures in our house including cockroaches and large soldier ants.

The basic beds in their frames were put up against the wall during the day, then pulled down at night. There was a large bed swing in the middle of the room. Further along at the end of the room was the 'kitchen area' where there were things like the matli, a large earthenware pot that held freshwater – again made by my Laduma. There were some pots and steel or aluminium sanis (plates) and small vadkis (bowls). There were a few treasured cups and saucers which came from Navsari, as for a brief time my Ajabapa had run a shop (funded by my Mum's Masa and Masi in South Africa) selling crockery. The walls were covered with chaan and every year as the bits crusted and fell off it would have to be redone and patched up (leape). My brother recalls goklas – little alcove areas in the wall in which to put divas and candles for light – as when we went to India there still was no electricity in Gujarat. By the time we left in the early 1960s, electrification was still in its preliminary stages with regional state electricity boards being rolled out across the vast country in stages. While we were in India there were often restricted periods of electricity. So for example, Suresh tells me he used to work late into the night as he could borrow books from school overnight but often would have to read by the light of a diva or candle as the electricity would go off. There were frequent power cuts, and it was not until 1970s that the situation improved. It was extremely basic, incomparable to Western standards, or even the standards available to a middle-class Indians in Munsad now.

The house had an upstairs (a bit like a loft) but that was mainly for storage, and there was a ladder at the edge of the room. It was also where the firewood for heating water pots and cooking was stored. We were all a bit scared to go up there. The nine months my Dad stayed in Munsad was spent on repairing and reinforcing the house as it was in a dilapidated state. Mum often recalls redoing the beams in the roof.

There was a room where we bathed with hot water which we boiled on a choolah. As described earlier, choolah were made by my Laduma, consisting of a pottery fire pit on which we cooked food and heated big pots for hot water for bathing. Toileting happened in the open, beyond our garden. Sanitation remains a challenge in India particularly in rural areas and it was always a hazardous challenge for women to find a private spot, whereas men would urinate and defecate more easily. It is still a hazard for much of the population and for women in particular who are vulnerable to sexual violence and abuse in all areas. It is a great concern in terms of public health and safety, and I wonder how sanitation is still such a challenge for a country which is now a superpower.

Laduma (Ma) used to keep a cow for milk. There was an unhappy incident involving Ma's calf, which we called Gongi, and was loved by us all. Maybe because she needed the money, Ma sold Gongi, but was swindled by a man who took her and did not pay the money promised. I know Ma was devastated as she loved her animals more than anything and little Gongi was her treasured animal. This incident shook us so profoundly that all of us in the family remember the event – although with our own version of what exactly happened. The one common theme was that my Ma was distraught by Gongi's loss but also by being swindled. This is not new in any of the worlds we live in, but it leaves the person swindled feeling humiliated and vulnerable.

Thinking about my Laduma, I feel that she had a quite a lonely life and that in some ways she might have preferred an insular life just with her animals. Getting caught up emotionally with family and friends was not for her. I cannot really say if Ma was close to anyone, be they family, friends, or neighbours. If I had my time again with her, I would like to think we would have tried to understand her better and be more considerate to her needs.

We kept chickens and once a year, after the egg-laying period had finished, a chicken was slaughtered for a chicken sak (curry). Despite being Hindus, our family were meat eaters, although we ate meat rarely and our diet was mainly vegetarian. The only time we ate meat was when visiting Navsari when my Ajabapa would on occasions make incredible meat kebabs with keema (minced mutton) and spices of chilli, garlic, ginger, and fragrant coriander pounded in a wooden pestle and a large heavy wooden mortar. This was finished off with homemade garam masala adding a distinct fragrance which my Mum captures in England with her homemade masala.

However, there was the once-a-year chicken dish that Mum made in Munsad using limited ingredients from the field for the sauce. Later in England, the Gujaratis and other Indians would go on to develop amazing sauces, creating richness by using more onions and tomatoes and fragrant spices, influenced by restaurant food and the availability and affordability of these vegetables. It remains our family's favourite food in my current multi-racial household and known to break periods of vegetarianism for at least one of my family members. In Munsad, our diet was very basic watery dahls, rotla and whatever vegetables Ma could gather from her small kandiya (plot). Rotlas are made from heavy sorghum flour and water, tapped into a flat pancake and cooked on tava (flat pan) and then popped on the open flame. This was a peasant-based diet. Rotla were heavier and more filling than rotli (chapatti) and made from wheat – these being a treat only made when visitors came. In England we would go on to eat rotlis every day.

My brothers and I attended the local village school. We were bright children and having come home from Nairobi and being born 'abroad' gave us some status.

Our names also added gravitas and had a poetic ring to it as Ma would shout it out to gather us for our dinner in the evenings. She would shout 'Suryakant... Chandrakant... Tara.... Come home, it's time to eat'. The neighbours would smile and say, 'old Laduma is after the kids.' Some of them remembered these evening callings in England, America and in India on my visits. They loved our Ma shouting out our names and it left an impression on many people in our village. This is because our names mean 'sun, moon and star' respectively and the endings to our name made them unique. Both Suresh and Chandra's name end in 'kant' and mine is 'mati'. They are masculine and feminine ending to our names used for formal occasions. Generally, the names end with 'bhai' for a male or 'ben' for a female. Ours are Suryakant (Surya or Suresh), Chandrakant (Chandra) and Taramati (Tara). Our names are based on astrological signs and usually determine the starting letter of the name. Both of my brothers' names are to that extent genuine and determined by my parents. My name according to the astrological signs should have started with a 'd' or an 'h'. My parents had asked a relative to register my name in Nairobi, as 'Hansa' (meaning a swan), but he decided that it really was absurd to call me anything but Tara....so going along with the planetary theme he had me registered as Taramati. Luckily my parents were happy with it and so am I as I cannot imagine being a swan! But Mum spent my early years telling me not to divulge that my name was not based on astrological signs. These signs were used to find a marriage partner and match for compatibility.

Luckily it was never a problem when marrying an English man called Peter from South London!

My Mum, on her own while Dad was in Kenya and England, was able to bring us up with more freedom and discretion than would have been possible if my Dad had been with us. I always felt a bit more privileged than other children in the village, and it was because Mum was young and dynamic. She must have grown in confidence by this stage, having had to survive without family support in Kenya. She had been an unhappy young woman with three small children living an enclosed life in Kenya. But moving back to India she was happier and more confident in her ability to manage the family and contribute to village life. So, in a strange way while poor Dad worked hard abroad, living and working in appalling conditions in England, the money he sent back home gave Mum some freedom. She was still incredibly young and a bit more of a city girl with access to her family only a short bus ride away in Navsari. That proximity to my Ajima and being able to support her was a major part of her happiness and gave her a vital role as the older sister with her siblings. Also, it cannot be ignored that the control my Dad would have exercised as her husband would certainly not have given her the opportunity to develop and grow in the way she did during these years in India. Seeing things from Mum's perspective, these were her years of great personal growth and confidence, and a sense of belonging after the isolation in Kenya. In many ways this was her 'golden age'. She was able to use her natural talents for the first time as a young woman on her 'home turf'. At Navratri and Diwali festivals and weddings she would take a lead in singing songs and dances, both in Navsari and Munsad. I remember her as having such a vibrant personality during these years when she was in her twenties.

Rukhimami (Maganmama's wife) and Mum had a strong bond. She came to stay with Mum in her flat in Leicester many years later

Mum went to Navsari often. When she stayed there overnight, I used to wait for her at the bus stop by a big tree called vad – a banyan tree with a wide evergreen canopy and a thick trunk. It was still there when I went in 1984 and is what I picture when I think of Munsad. The banyan is native to the subcontinent and is India's national tree. Suresh also described how he would hate Mum being away on occasions when he felt unwell with his asthma. I am not sure how often she stayed away but to us as children it left an impression. It may have also been because we loved being in Navsari as it had a lively atmosphere compared to sleepy Munsad, so with Mum staying away it meant we were missing out. I remember Navsari with rose-tinted glasses but Suresh, being older, remembers more of the details.

Kishormama, Chandra and Suresh as boys

Suresh was the same age as our uncle Kishormama - as mentioned earlier both uncle and nephew were born about the same time, but in different countries.

He recalls just going here, there and everywhere with the uncles. He said their house was made from kamri (thin wood) so actually not as solid as ours in Munsad, but to him, it felt more luxurious. He says that to him there was an air of being on holiday as there was always an element of excitement with so much going on. But he said he did not like the evenings because he recalls Ajabapa being drunk and there being much fighting arising from that. He recalls that we all slept on the floor when visiting and going out with Kishormama to get daru (alcohol) for Ajabapa. In the morning things would be calm and Ajabapa would be kind and take us out for something to eat or to drink tadi (fermented date juice which was rather sour and tasted like rough cider) – but it was all such a treat. I think despite the tension and the rows Suresh rarely wanted to go back home to our quiet village.

Ajima was also a strong character and, as I have described, was a natural networker and a bit of 'queen bee.' She did have charisma and flair, and I saw much more of that side to her when I revisited India for the first time in 1984 and saw her through adult eyes.

Ravji Ranchod (Ajabapa), Tara, Kuvarben (Ajima).
My Mum had this photo taken before we left India as she did have a similar studio photo of herself with her maternal grandparents which she loved.

Our other uncle Maganmama was handsome and kind, and overly generous considering he did not have material wealth. Suresh remembers him taking us out and treating us to delicious street food. He recalls Maganmama taking him to a workshop where he would carve figurines for the religious festivals taking place. He can also remember going to

Maganmama's marriage to Rukhimami, which took place in the night with lamps (farnas) and the jan, which is the wedding party dancing to the bride's home. I think I can remember that too but weddings in India from that era blur into one. It is hard to differentiate one wedding from another from my memories as a young child. With Kishormama, Suresh would also go to the 'Vasant Talkies' to see Bollywood films.

Suresh felt Manekmama and Kantumama were subject to greater violence from my Ajabapa, that is how he remembers it. But on the positive side Suresh can remember when Manekmama started tailoring and then later started diamond cutting. He recalls going with Ajima near the Ashram where he moved to start diamond cutting. Ajima had to pay money upfront for the apprenticeship. It was the result of Ajima's networks that Manekmama was able to find this opportunity. One gets a sense that my Ajima was always on the lookout for opportunities of good marriage for her daughters and good jobs for her sons.

The diamond cutting trade took off in Navsari after we left India, and the fortunes of the family changed quite dramatically as a result. Manekmama was instrumental in helping the family to move to a purpose-built three-storey home, housing the three family households and my Ajima. Maganmama unfortunately died young from kidney disease, leaving behind a widow, our Rukhimami and four children. Kantumama later became a medical student in India but died tragically young from stomach cancer. All the older male siblings greatly loved and respected Mum as she had been so involved in helping bring them up when they were tiny and had endured and shared a life marred by poverty, addiction and violence. As an older sister she helped Ajima to manage the chaos and was her close confidante. We were as a result indulged, and it is no wonder that we loved being in Navsari.

I was two years old when Dad returned to Kenya. Suresh says we were always conscious our father was abroad, and he was not aware of any other significant male figures in our family in Munsad. Icchabapa was the only male figure (kaka my Dad's uncle) who was strict and domineering. We tried to avoid him so as not to get scolded or receive physical punishment. He was a bully and would use any excuse to belittle us. Suresh says although he knew we were related and part of the kutumb so whilst Icchabapa had some control over us, he never felt that he was 'our family'. He appreciated they were the older generation, and we were lower down in the pecking order. At times, he says, we would complain to Ma and Mum, but we tried not to cross his path as he did seem to have the ultimate male authority over us. Later in Wembley, London, Suresh would stay with his son Lallubhai (we called him Kakuji – a variation of kaka) and his family while he was doing his City and Guilds course. He had six children, who all lived in London, but the three daughters married and moved to America and Canada. Kakuji's brother Narotambhai (known as 'little uncle' by us as he was the younger one, so Nana) lived in Leicester with his wife, our Nani and their family of five children Both these families had come over from Uganda in the 1970's. We had a lot to do with all these relatives over the years. Kakuji, his wife our Kaki, and their son and a daughter have sadly died as have our Nana and Nani.

Our immediate neighbours in Munsad were incredibly important to us. Dhanima had had something happen to her in childbirth and walked bent over and with her hands on her knees. Mum says she just could not stand after the birth of her last child. She had four children, Pushpa, Gopal, Niru and Naran. Gopalbhai went away to study but when he was around, he was

extremely popular and seemed progressive. Niruben was my protector and would take me out. Whenever Mum smacked or scolded me, she would intervene to protect me. I just remember we had fun with them, and we were popular with their family. I enjoyed dancing and showing off and our neighbours encouraged me to be the centre of attention by getting me to perform.

Tara aged 4

Gopalbhai was very encouraging to all of us and to our Mum when we were in India. Naranbhai would take Suresh and Chandra out. They were as significant as any of our relatives in years to come. Pushpaben, Gopalbhai and Naranbhai moved to America and Niruben to Blackburn, England.

I went and stayed with Gopalbhai's family in Baltimore on route to a conference in Connecticut. I stayed for a few days with them and visited Washington. Gopalbhai became a civil engineer but also had a motel that his wife ran; by similar means other Asian families in America made extra money. It must have been hard running a motel, but many did this as well as pursuing a career to get their children the best private education. They had four daughters. When I visited, they told me they were all in the 'gifted and talented' stream at their school. I was using a couple of days travelling to and from Washington sightseeing and visiting the Smithsonian. They were confused as to why I was in the country without my children. I explained I was a Lecturer in a British University, and part of my job was to present a paper at a conference, but they did not understand that it was an academic role. When they realised it was a teaching job at a university, they said I was a 'Professor' and not a Lecturer. In American terms they were right although I explained that in the British system being a professor was higher up the academic career ladder. Still, they were impressed by my role and that I was attending the conference in America while my two little daughters were in England with their daddy. I told them it was hard to combine a career and bring up children as much of the childcare and other arrangements still fell on the mother. Also, the childcare system in Britain was not adequate or well-resourced by the state to support working parents. They said they were inspired, so I felt positive that they might see me as a good role model. On return from my conference, as I juggled childcare, with teaching, writing and research with all the domestic demands as well as childcare (as Peter was often working abroad), I hoped I had not set up those girls to thinking they could 'have it all'. All the girls grew up and did very well academically, and I know they now have careers and families of their own. I hope they had a decent support structure.

Niruben was incredibly supportive and kind to us as we were growing up in England and I remember staying with her after my Dad died. They took me to Blackpool and to the Zoo. They bought me a skirt and a top as traditionally people gave clothes when parents died to help in practical ways. I still remember the yellow crimplene blouse with a black and mauve skirt.

When Dhanima came to England to visit, Mum was delighted to see her. She had moved from India to live with Gopalbhai and his family in America and it must have been very hard for her away from her homeland. The alternative would have been for her to live alone in Munsad. I often wonder which option was better for older people – to move with the family or stay in the homeland. She too has died now. Although Dhanima was living with her family, my Mum feels it was not a good life for her in America as she was severely disabled, and Mum feels she was very lonely, alienated and unhappy. The impact of migration on older people was harsh if they were left in India on their own or harsh even amongst the family if encouraged to join the family abroad.

It is very strange to think we used to huddle in tiny dark houses, living in our village in India, talking, and eating popcorn together during heavy rains in the monsoon season – but we then end up living in various parts of the globe. I often recall those moments with nostalgia, even now. Although I realise how little actual time we all spent together in the grand scheme of things, they left a lasting impression and created a special bond in our relationships. I wrote a piece for the Guardian supplement about the ritual of making popcorn around times of heavy rain. It did not get published because it did not contain a recipe, but I will share an excerpt as I believe it conveys a valuable memory, and a ritual passed on from that experience to my daughters.

> *During monsoon, it would be dark, and damp and all the neighbours would come around to while away the time with our family. Our friends and cousins would all come, and we would scramble to get a place on the swing bed, some of us teetering off the edge! During these periods of rainy season my mother would pop a pan over the choolah, add some oil and throw in corn kernels gathered and dried from the fields. The sound of popping corn and*

rain; the warm aroma filled with chatter and excitements of us kids; the rain lashing against the trees and creating a river along the road and the occasional charge of electricity accompanied by thunder – is one of the loveliest memories of those early years of my life. We would all share the popcorn, ranging from the very young to the very old. The women would all tell stories.

My mother, brothers and I did join our father in England 45 years ago. So, when my daughters were very small, I too made them popcorn whenever it rained hard and thundered and I recalled to them my childhood memories of popcorn eating. My daughters are now aged 18 and 16 and always associate popcorn eating and sharing with rainy weather.

Recently my mother came to see us with her brother and sister-in-law, who were visiting from India. They were surprised when my eldest daughter presented them with a large bowl of popcorn just as the heavens opened on a July afternoon. Her Ma (my mother), on making the connection was very impressed that my early experiences had transcended across the generations and across culturally with her dual heritage Indian/English grandchildren. She tucked into her popcorn with the satisfaction of a matriarch who had passed on the ritual that is likely to continue into another generation albeit popped in a microwave on a rainy July in Bristol.

[Submitted to Saturday Guardian – Family Supplement 1st November 2008.]

Gopalbhai's eldest daughter did a doctorate and married a Vietnamese refugee. All his four daughters married across different ethnicities and cultures in America creating such diversity. The cross fertilisation of education, cultures, and backgrounds within a fleeting period of history just in our extended family and amongst our immediate neighbours is extraordinary.

Back in Munsad, we played with everyone and anyone outside our houses. However, there was a gatekeeping system in the form of the older women who would not let people into their homes. So, the caste system was robust and applied to us too. In our village, like so many, there were many people who were at the time known in derogatory terms such as 'untouchables.' Now it is more appropriate, and is their preferred term, to refer to their community as Dalits. They were poorer in all respects and lived in jupadis or tents and shacks. They had no real rights or protection as a caste when we were there. The whole microcosm of Indian society was reflected in Munsad, from high-ranking Brahmins to the poorest members of the caste hierarchy, including Parsis, who had migrated as Muslims years ago from Iran. The Hindu caste system was strong then, as it is now. We too experienced discrimination from people who perceived themselves as higher caste; Suresh recalls running through a house in Munsad with a friend whose mother stopped him and sprinkled water over him to purify her house, since a tainted individual of lower caste had entered her premises. The fact he can remember that speaks volumes.

Apart from the caste hierarchy we were lucky to have a father who, despite his own hardship, was sending us money, so we never felt that we did not know where the next meal was coming from. To that extent we were better off, compared to some of our relatives. Our Diwalima's family was a single parent household and did not know where and when they would eat next. Vallabhai, her son, always told Suresh that we would get to England, but he, Vallabhai, was not convinced he would ever go abroad. In years to come he did visit us in England and is settled in America now. As recounted elsewhere, they have all, except the eldest brother and his son, ended up abroad. But Vallabhai was right, we were destined to go to England even though at times we felt that it would never happen.

Ready to leave India

By December 1962 when I had just turned seven, my Dad had made plans to send for us. None of us siblings can really remember details of our preparations except there was pickling and preparation of food to take to England. Included in this was the making of papad – we later discovered that they were called 'popadoms' in England. The making of papad took place with the help of the neighbourhood women. It was a communal task as it required different skills from contributors and was a labour-intense activity.

Women made dough with urad flour which is hard to mix - especially in enormous quantities. The mixture had to be stiff and elastic and not at all like a bread dough. Eventually, it would be stretched and re-stretched to form smooth logs about three to four centimetres in diameter. They were put into huge mounds and smoothed over with oil to stop them drying. Then they were cut into thin rounds bound by a string which had one end attached to someone's big toe and the other end held in the hand, acting like a knife to cut a perfect circle about half a centimetre thick. These little discs were rolled out on a large steel plate and women and young girls would sit around rolling them with a wooden rolling pin, which we call a velan. This rolling pin, also used for rolling rotii, was bulbous in the middle but narrowed at each end helping to get the papad thin depending on how much pressure was put on the dough at various angles. Young girls would roll out the first stage of the papad disc, then it would pass on to the older women who would take those medium discs and work their magic to roll out into paper-thin papad, which would then be lifted off the upside-down steel plates onto which they had been rolled. Then they would put the papad carefully into shallow baskets until they had about six or seven. Old cotton and voile saris were laid outside in the yard and the papad would be laid out to dry in the fierce heat of the sun. This job usually started early and finished by the early afternoon as the drying had to be completed by the time the sun set. It was hard graft, but one filled with gossip, stories, singing and camaraderie amongst the women helping each other with this seasonal task, or for celebratory occasions - including preparation for migration and taking a large bundle to England. At times of weddings, making papad for a wedding party would happen months ahead, and the activity would be filled with wedding songs and aunties making crude jokes about the groom and wife to be or the in-laws! I aways remember these occasions of communal activities with joy and happiness. It was a women-centred activity that I loved as we would all have a role in the papad making process whatever our age.

I remember Mum got frocks made for me as Manekmama was also a women's tailor. I do not think Mum realised that we were going to end up in England during one of the worst winters in living memory, so my cotton dresses were not the most appropriate. There just seemed to be all kinds of preparation for taking non-perishable foods such as chevdo, tickhi puris, salted cumin biscuits and paunk (made from roasted millet). There were Indian sweetmeats and halwa to offer friends, wadi made from fenugreek which had been pulped and dried to eat back in England, and bhoomla ('Bombay Duck') which was dried fish. All these things were at least transportable and easily reconstituted with spices into 'curries' as Indian food was scarce back in England. We also took spices and masala ground up and ready for use such as garam masala and dhana jeeru, a combination widely used by Gujaratis for vegetables. For people migrating to England later this was not such a concern as shops were supplying a variety of groceries even by the late 60s. But in the late 50's and early 60's there was little choice, so if you were travelling by a ship then you tended to take everything you possibly could. As a part of the preparations Mum bought bedding in the form of a silk rajai. I remember it was light green with an apricot border. It was like a quilt and was hand stitched to keep it together using simple running stitch in a pattern. Years later, I saw something like that on display at an Indian textile exhibition at the V & A Museum in London. I know that our rajai incurred a stain from a house painting project, and in the end, we gave it away to a charity shop maybe 50 years after our migration. When I saw the exhibition about the textiles from Gujarat and it featured rajais in different designs, I wish we had taken better care and held on to ours.

Ajima made a huge vat of mango and lime pickles and put them in a large pickling banee - a large earthenware glazed jar. Ajabapa had made a wooden frame to protect it when it was loaded on and off the ship. I remember our embarrassment at Tilbury Docks as the banee came off the ship and we saw the thick, treacly, spicy pickling oil running out of the broken jar, which despite Ajabapa's best efforts had split at its final unceremonious unloading. Even in the cold and confusion it was the first of many embarrassing situations we are never to forget, especially as people stepped in it and the red oily juice was carried on the soles of the travellers. The chewdo, jeera and tikhi puris packed in our cabin as snacks came in very handy on the ship as we hated all the food on offer, even though it was Christmas, and my Dad had presumably paid for us to have meals. These dried snacky foods Mum had packed were our salvation.

I cannot remember clearly the details of leaving, but we when were all packed up, we first went to Navsari and then to Bombay. I cannot remember saying goodbye to anyone and just vaguely recall climbing up onto the ship and seeing the wobbly ladder that led to the entrance door. It was a long way down to the bottom to the water and a bit scary. I do recall Ajabapa helping us find the cabin and settling us. He said if anyone comes up to you just shrug your shoulders and say, "No speak English". It was true, we did not!

The P&O ticket for our passage to England

When I imagine us boarding the ship, I get confused by having watched the film 'Titanic'. We were not in the equivalent of steerage, but we were a long way down in the ship. I wish I could remember how I felt as our ship moved off. Most people were not travelling to a new country but were just having a cruise to England for Christmas. We were with a handful of South Asian travellers. As well as us, there was another Gujarati family, and a Muslim family. There was also a Marathi woman (from the State of Maharashtra in western India) who spoke English and who tried to tell us about dinner and meals. She was a professional woman and seemed very cultured compared to us. The rest of us Indian travellers were all on the same table and none of us knew how to use knives and forks. I am not sure any of us really liked the food. I know I lived on eggs and tomatoes. The Goan waiter looking after us felt deeply sorry for me and tried to get me 'curry.' In my excitement I thought he said kudhi.

Kudhi is a yogurt based spicy runny sauce usually eaten with mori dahl (dahl with just cumin, salt, and bit of turmeric) and rice with a spinach accompaniment. The smell of the 'curry', an early version of the 'Vesta' brand did not help with my sea sickness and my wish to be at home. It was horrible. We spent a lot of time holed up in our cabin. Once seasickness abated, we explored the ship a little. We did not go to the swimming pool, attend children's parties, or attend any of the entertainment laid on. We felt out of place then, but if we were on a cruise ship now at Christmas, I am sure we would make the most of what was on offer. It was a preparation of how we would feel for years to come in England: the wrong people in the wrong place.

We were on the ship for about 17 days. Suresh made an interesting observation about the journey in that we were wearing shoes all the time since leaving India rather than being barefoot; coupled with regular washing of our whole bodies meant the thorns and little bits lodged in the soles of our feet gradually all came out, so by the time we arrived on land our feet were soft and unblemished. I am sure it felt very satisfying.

The P & O cruise ship SS Stratheden

We travelled through the Mediterranean, stopped in Aden where Mum bought a watch and a bottle of jasmine perfume. Then through the Suez Canal. There was a delay to our journey as I believe we had to rescue another ship in trouble (but it could be another confusion in my mind with fiction); however, I am sure that it took longer to get to England than scheduled because of it.

Meanwhile the 'big freeze' had arrived on Christmas Eve in England just as we were leaving India. January 1963, when we arrived remains one of the coldest months in central England with average temperatures below freezing at -2.1 degrees centigrade, and this lasted well into March. Our ship arrived into ice and drifts of snow, and the country was trying to deal with this exceptional weather. It was bitter, and Mum's sari and cardigan were no protection from the biting cold, nor was my summer dress or my brothers' thin trouser suits. I had imagined for years that our Dad would come running up to us and scoop us into his arms. It did not happen like that, and the welcome when we saw him and my Balwantbhai was more reserved.

My Dad looked ill, and we were all freezing. They were sorting out baggage and Dad had luckily borrowed duffle coats from the neighbour's children. We remember getting into a taxi they had hired. The white taxi man did these runs for Asian families and was well regarded by the community. My brothers remember him telling them to look out for bridges and count them on route to Leicester. The roads were full of snow piled high on either side of the roads. When we arrived at our new home there was snow everywhere in the little street.

My Dad had lodgers - Dullabhai came out to help but slipped in the snow. His wife Dhaibhabhi had made us hot rotlis and sak. The living room where we sat had a coal burning fire with a large black range. In one compartment was the rotii in a neat stack for all the hungry mouths. We all sat by the fire and watched the screen on a black and white TV which was enthralling. We had never seen a working television, and my brothers and I believe we saw an episode of Coronation Street that first evening in Wingfield Street. The coal fire was just magical and the only heating in an otherwise cold room. However, we all enjoyed this first decent meal in weeks - on land. It also dawned on us that this was our new home.

We had left all our relatives behind, and I did not know then, but I would never see my Laduma or Bhulima ever again.

PART 2: 1963 – 1974

This covers the period of our early life in Leicester. Our experiences of settling into the new life in a cold climate, both physically and emotionally. Race, racism, and aspects of resistance to it runs through this part including touching on 'mixed race' relationship in that period and the interchange of how I harnessed my energy in addressing aspects of anti-racism and discrimination in my work, and developing partnerships with others later in my career. The impact of racism on us is addressed throughout.

I explore aspects of our living arrangements including homelife, food, play, friendships, and relationships with our early Asian communities. I move on to my Dad's stroke at age of 42 and its impact on our family, and his death six years later.

The early days of education and the role of supplementary schools, social life, secondary school education (comprehensive and secondary modern), class, culture, gender, marriages, and the response by our communities including the arrival, contribution and impact of East African Asians. I focus on further education in the sixth form to illustrate my short experience of the grammar school system. Our relationship with old neighbours and extended families in Leicester and beyond. And finally, us all leaving to go on to higher education outside our city.

Early days in Leicester

Days after we arrived in Leicester, Dad fell at work and was taken to hospital. He had come to England with some underlying health concerns and our cold, poor overcrowded living conditions exacerbated the situation. It was almost as if he had kept himself together physically, got us over to England and he could just let go of all the balls he had been juggling in the air! It was the start of years of ill health to follow, but at that point there were so many emotional and practical difficulties to cope with, including us starting school, the awfulness of the winter and negotiating our way round the health system. Luckily my cousin Balwantbhai lived with us and he was able to help.

My Mum did not really have proper clothing for the dire winter of 1963. Fortunately, she was given some winter boots which she wore with her sari, a coat and headscarf. I do not think she wore thick tights under her petticoat. My cousin took her to the hospital to see Dad on the bus. It must have been scary and daunting and very cold without the right clothes. We all wore inadequate apparel because we could not afford appropriate clothing, and culturally people had to conform to traditional clothes (sari and salwar kameez if you were a Punjabi woman, and turbans for Sikh men). Muslim women in those days did not wear any face coverings such as the hijab as far as I recall, although almost all Asian women, including my Mum, covered their hair in the presence of men and the older generation as a mark of respect. The inappropriate clothing, as I saw it as a child, just made us stand out in our neighbourhood and I hated it for that reason.

Those early years were so difficult, and I often felt that in the hierarchy of prejudice we had the worst experience amongst migrants 'of colour', in that we stood out because of our religion, being non-Christian, our food being so 'smelly and foreign' because of our spices and speaking in a very different language in which even our alphabet looked so strange against the western one. At the time, other groups and communities like the African Caribbeans from Jamaica and other islands did share English as their native tongue, they wore what we termed 'English' clothes and most attended churches so had a similar recognisable faith. To some extent, I felt envious of them and their commonality with the majority, even though they undoubtedly experienced racism – somehow the words 'wogs' and 'paki' were much more than us being 'coloured.' They conveyed contempt for our culture, food and religion, and us as a people. It was a statement of more than the colour of our skin. I was very aware of all things that labelled me as 'foreign' in the eyes of white people. Although as a child we did wear western clothes, it would be summer dresses with coats and cardigans and headscarf! Why did our parents put silk headscarves on us as young girls and not woolly hats? I really could not understand, but it would have been so useful to help us blend in, or so I thought. Also, woolly tights instead of socks might have helped keep us warm. The socks just came to the knees and kept falling as they were cheap and didn't have good elastic. I know we only had one pair of shoes, so they were school shoes, and no boots in the winter. It was partly that our parents could not afford things, partly ignorance and the chaotic life we all had to survive as independent members of the family. To an extent we just had to accept and adapt to whatever our parents said as we were never allowed to voice our opinions. I am sure we could have put them straight on a few things if allowed to.

Mum had to negotiate the buses on her own very quickly to visit my Dad at the hospital. She did not speak a word of English - I cannot imagine how she managed, but she did. How did Mum get to the hospital without getting lost? How did she manage to understand money? I am still unclear who took care of the basics in the very early days of Dad getting ill. I know we were registered for schools. My brothers started school at Mellor Junior, and because I was just seven, I went to Ellis Avenue Infant school. The school itself was daunting and even in early days, I remember we were on the end of racism daily. Initially, we were called 'wogs' incessantly at school and we knew it was a term of abuse, but like many others we just accepted that is how it would be. I stuck around with one or two other Indian children. I was lucky that my friend Shanti had just arrived to join her family in England. They lived around the corner from our house. Her parents had left her in India with her grandma when they first migrated - it was a widespread practice in those days to bring the sons initially but leave the girls behind. It was cruel but many parents did not want their girls to be corrupted by western permissiveness and wanted to see how things would pan out. I was always grateful that Dad did not tell Mum to leave me behind.

The 1948 Nationality Act had granted UK citizenships to citizens of Britain's colonies and former colonies. The British passports gave us all a right to come to Britain and stay. Since 1958, there were anti-Black riots and resentment by the white British population. Both the Conservatives and Labour Governments were reacting to the racial tensions - some real, and some perceived. Having supported the initial move to get more workers over to rebuild post war Britain from the Caribbean and former colonies, the British Government were now worried it was causing social unrest by the white British feeling threatened by a Black and Asian presence. In sending us our passage to England, Dad was responding to the new Commonwealth Immigration Act 1962 which was trying to restrict entry to those with passports issued in Britain. It was also a racialised Act in that it was trying to stop the 'coloured migration' – an expression commonly used at the time.

To put the numbers in context this is a useful reminder of what was happening:

> *Amid the rising chorus of demands for immigration control, the voice of reason could still be heard. Labour party chairman Tom Driberg told the Trades Union Congress [said]:*
>
> *'People talk about a colour problem arising in Britain. How can there be colour problem here? Even after all the immigration of the past few years, there are only 190,000 coloured people in our population of over 50 million – that is, only four out of every 1,000. The real problem is not black skins, but white prejudice.'*
>
> [Staying Power, the History of Black People in Britain, Peter Fryer (1984)]

The new legislation had functioned as an incentive to get us all over quickly and it was evident that my Dad's health and finances were not in a great state, but the fact that he saved enough for us to come over and to buy a house was remarkable on his limited income. At the time families and friends from our community were starting to gather and were borrowing from each other, rather than the banks. This was the way all the Asian communities purchased initial properties. My Dad bought our dilapidated house for £650 with saved and borrowed money. This was also partly due to racism, which made access to a mortgage from banks difficult. Had that been easier, or an option, he may have been able to buy a house in a better condition. But needs must and most Asian families could not wait for the ideal moment to get their family to join them in England or to find solutions to housing.

Shanti had lived in India for four years with her grandmother and had not seen her mum, dad or brothers, and had even missed the birth of her new brother - who was a baby when she arrived. In some ways the new act did galvanise many fathers/husbands from the subcontinent to bring their daughters, children and relatives over to England quickly.

At Infant School, the expectation was that parents of the pupils would drop off and pick up their infants from the school gates. This concept made no sense to my family as my brothers were allowed to go to school on their own – clearly not understanding that in this country there was some duty of care for young children under eight years of age. Our parents were too burdened by the process of just arriving and surviving, and negotiating life without adequate money or language and just getting by with the basics. 'Duty of care' as seen by schools was a concept unfamiliar to them.

In the early days, I was picked up from the infant school, but it was touch and go whether Mum came, or our lodger, Dhaibhabhi. She had a baby so she would come with him in the pram. There were times that I was waiting by the school gates with a teacher (annoyed and agitated, as it happened often) until Mum or Dhaibhabhi turned up. I had not learnt to be embarrassed by being the last to go home. Mum did not take it seriously that I was considered too young to walk home by myself because in India I had walked everywhere in the locality on my own. By our Indian village standard, they thought it was mollycoddling. However, she was also busy trying to make sense of life in England with her husband in hospital. Meanwhile, my brothers were shown a route of how to get to their school on the first day by Balwantbhai. Suresh spent all morning concentrating on remembering the route. He was supposed to bring Chandra home with him for lunch, but he was concentrating so hard on remembering the route home that Suresh completely forgot to pick him up and went home on his own. There were a lot of those mishaps but somehow we did just get on with it.

We were later so careful with the needs of our own children growing up and especially with schools. But in the grand scheme of things, we can understand that their priorities were appropriate in context of those times. We always appreciated our parents had made great sacrifices to get us here in this country in the way they did. We were expected to take responsibilities, and childhood was not an excuse for not doing so.

It was the stuff of early migration – we all went through similar experiences. We didn't have the language to communicate at all, and the state institutions were unsympathetic and antagonistic to all of us who came from India and Pakistan. We were out of our depth and our lives were so alien and different to the one we had left in India that it was incomprehensible. How did we navigate this strange new world in one of the harshest winters in living memory? As the youngest and the only girl in my family, my closest companion was Shanti. I shared a bedroom with my brothers - they were in a three-quarter sized bed and me in a single bed. I missed my Mum at nights, as I had slept with her in India, and I regularly complained about tummy ache at night so I could sleep with her. Amazingly, Dad would just allow me to come in with them and not scold me. We had so many people living with us, some were lodgers but some closely related family members.

Our old, terraced house was in a ridiculously small street just off Shaftesbury Avenue. We had three rooms upstairs (with no bathroom) and three rooms downstairs including the kitchen. The middle room downstairs had a huge cast iron range for cooking with lots of compartments in which we kept our rotlis hot. In some ways there was companionship for Mum with the only other woman, who was Dhaibhabhi. She lived with her husband, and her baby son in our front room which was the room entered from the pavement through the front door. It was called the 'parlour' by our white neighbours. My Dad's older brother, Chaganbapa, came to England from Kenya and was living with us after we arrived. He was a great one for reciting 'The Mahabharat' and recounting stories from the Ramayan – our ancient Hindu texts. Stories of

Arjun and Panch Pandavas rang through the upstairs front bedroom. Storytelling was a wonderful way of bonding. We would all gather in the upstairs front bedroom and Dayaramkaka would be smoking his pipe; the room would be full of men who had worked all day talking and sharing stories. Most endured racism and sharing stories in the evening was a way to connect and feel less alienated. We three children would listen amongst the smoke and the fumes of kerosene from the paraffin heater. Often it lulled me to sleep before it was bedtime - for this reason I cannot remember any of the stories.

My brothers were influenced by my uncle, Chaganbapa, and his words as my Dad was not particularly religious or interested in recounting tales. Dad did believe in God, but he was not one for devotional adoration or temple worship. Chaganbapa used to pose philosophical questions to the men, and my brothers liked being part of the male tribe. At one time soon after we arrived, there were eight adults and four children living in this little house with only an outside toilet and one coal fire downstairs for heating, but also the dangerous paraffin heaters. I am filled with fear, thinking about what an unacceptable safety issue it would be now, with children, dangerous petrol and fire hazards. There was linoleum in all rooms so no carpets. Sleeping with your day clothes on was often the only way to stay warm with the obvious hot water bottle. The lack of hot running water made things exceedingly difficult. Ice on the inside of the windows and lack of appropriate clothing in the winter meant we were always cold.

Mum was taken by Dhaibhabhi to the public baths in Cossington Street. Later we would go together every Friday evening. I remember the smell of the place and sounds of the bath water running out of huge taps as it flowed into the 'the slipper bath'. The place smelt of chlorine and the hot steam mixed with the noise of women talking and shouting. Mum and I shared the bath, and she would firstly wash my exceptionally long thick hair as well as her own in clean water, then wash us both down; that would be a week's worth of dirt to wash off. It was a purposeful activity and there was a logical ritual. No relaxing or soaking in the tub. There was an allocated time with no opportunity to dry our hair. Mum used to tie my hair in a ponytail, and it would drip and make my back all wet. Sometimes if we had to go into a shop, the women serving us would tell my Mum to get me home in case 'I caught my death of cold'. We did not have washing machines, and I still remember Mum washing clothes outside in the yard on stone floor (like in India) and trying to dry them in the 'entry' which provided the back entrances to these terraced houses. I can picture the clothes on the line against the wall of the entry, but often they were like cardboard because of the freezing air. This went on for years and I still cannot fathom out why we did not use the laundrettes. Maybe it was considered alien, or it was another place we had to expose ourselves to our white neighbours when it was not essential to do so. It was also the place where racism could be experienced through putting our clothes in machines which white people would find offensive to use after us. Also, if money could be saved in any way, then use of hard physical work was often the preferred substitute.

Dad at work

Dad recovered and came home and went back to work in a backroom workshop of a gents' tailor shop in city centre. Leicester was the centre of textile and hosiery trade with numerous small workplaces. I do not think it allowed for a harmonious environment for

Dad as the work was based on 'piecework', so he laboured long hours, including bringing work home to earn more. The English-speaking women seamstresses at work were often rude and unkind, but he really had to handle that because he could not have done more physically demanding manual work outside. Also, he loved the fact that he had a 'profession' and stayed put. It must have been difficult working in a small basement workshop where he could not participate in the banter and camaraderie of the workplace. He worked for a couple of different shops before he had a stroke in 1966.

Family photo of us after the wedding of Balwantbhai to Susheila. L to R: back row Mum, Nanima, Susheilabhabhi, Balwantbhai. Front row: Suresh, Tara, Chandra, Chaganbapa, Dad

Our lodgers moved out bit by bit including Dullabbhai and Dhaibhabhi who bought their own house and moved out with their little son Champack. Dayaramkaka and his son moved out eventually and bought their own house too, and Dad's brother Chaganbapa, his wife Nanima and his son (our cousin Balwantbhai) moved into their own house in Coral Street where Balwantbhai and Susheilabhabhi still live to this day. Balwantbhai had an arranged marriage to Susheilabhabhi, and they brought up their three children in that house. We were very involved with their children Dilip, Usha, and Kiran as they grew up.

We loved looking after them and watching them grow – they were one of our nearest blood relatives in Leicester. Many relatives were settling along Belgrave Road and in time this would become a thriving centre for my community.

For years Chaganbapa and Nanima lived together with three generations in the house. Chaganbapa died in his sixties and Nanima lived much longer, helping with the children growing up. In her old age she moved to a nursing home when she became frail. By this time moving older frail relatives out of the family home had become part of a social change taking place in Asian families across Britain and especially in places like Leicester. I will explore this later in Part 3.

We then had another lodger with us living on his own, waiting to save money to get his wife over to England. He worked the night shift at Walkers Crisp Factory and had the little bedroom which most people converted to an indoor bathroom. Dad did not want to lose a bedroom so started to convert the coal shed into an outside shower room which ran off an old Ascot water heater he had installed in the kitchen. The Ascot was a godsend as it gave us hot water at the sink. The workers who were supposed to plaster the walls did half a job and disappeared. I remember my brothers tried to find out what happened to them, but they took our money, leaving the job unfinished. Eventually, we had to pay someone else to finish the job and tile it.

By the time the outside bathroom became a rudimentary shower room, I had to follow one of two scenarios. The daytime scenario, when we were not expecting visitors (rare as people were always popping round), I would put on an oversized nylon housecoat that our next-door neighbour, Mrs Overhead, gave us one Christmas. She gave it to us for Mum and me to share, as she could see us running from the coal shed into the house from her upstairs window. I would put on the housecoat and run through the house and into the backyard and into the coal shed. It would be cold, so I would put the shower on and wait for the steam to cloud up and warm up the space. The light switch was inside (a safety hazard), and I would often see a line of snails lurking in the damp and around corners of the room. The trick was to have a shower as fast as possible and wash my long thick hair, dry off with the towel hanging on a nail and not tread on any snails! I would collect the clothes, and if I was lucky, I could slip out through the yard into the kitchen, through the sitting room and rush upstairs to the bedroom, then take my time in getting dressed and drying off properly in peace.

Evening scenarios were different in that people were all around, and for us women it was not acceptable to be going off to the 'shower' with a housecoat, so we had to go with all our clothes, repeat the sequence above, but avoid even more snails at that time of the day and follow the above sequence but put all the clothes on in the wet room. The dress etiquette for men was not as strict and they could walk out from the shower room with just a towel round their waist. But Mum, my brothers and I still remember those snails.

It was incredible that our neighbours Mr and Mrs Overhead never complained and in fact Mrs Overhead tried to be helpful by giving us a housecoat. I do not know what they made of all the steam coming out from the top and bottom of the room as it was only a shed door which stood between the shower room and the yard. Mrs Overhead was the only person who gave us Christmas presents, and even though we did not celebrate the festival, it was exciting to get a gift that we could open, especially something practical. Although it was a bit of a palaver bathing in the converted coal shed, it was preferable to going to the public baths. Mrs Overhead's son was a 'teddy boy' for a time, and although scary and notorious to many, in person he seemed more into his outfits rather than presenting a threat. In those days of fierce racism, we could not have asked for better neighbours. They were good working-class people who were trying to adjust to their changing neighbourhood, and this must have been challenging for them too.

Suresh, Chandra (holding Dad's bike) and Tara: outside Mrs. Overhead's house

Playtime and leisure

The early days saw me dashing off to Shanti's and playing with her, as her household was a bit easier going than ours. My brothers were friendly with her brothers, but I cannot remember them going to their house often. We would play in her yard which was larger than ours – an elastic band game, skipping ropes and a five-pebble finger game called 'snobs'.

Sometimes we played with her doll. Although our immediate neighbours, the Overheads, were good to us, the others were not so tolerant. One day Shanti and I were playing with her doll on the steps of No.10 in my street and Mr Tee opened the door. We knew their surname as they had 'Tee' displayed on their door. He shouted at us, and we moved away leaving the doll on his steps out of sheer fear. He kicked the doll across the street. It was the time of ferocious racism and people started to be physically abusive, fuelled by the coverage of 'coloured immigrants' and inflammatory rhetoric by politicians like Enoch Powell, famously in his 'Rivers of Blood' speech. I do not think Shanti and I talked about the incident, but we never sat on his doorstep ever again. His wife, Mrs Tee, was friendly, but her husband turned against us over the years, and they moved away like many white families in our street and the neighbourhood. As our street was exceedingly small, it did not even feature in the A – Z of Leicester. There were three houses on our side with a factory next door, and eight houses across the other side.

Tara and Shanti playing in her yard

Tara and Shanti

Suresh and I visited our old street in 2024, and the old house looked vastly different. It had been modernised and was for sale. The outside toilet and the coal shed were knocked down and the kitchen extended into the rest of the yard. There was no outside space, and the house sold for over £300,000. The entry door still looked as if it had been unpainted since we were there. One of the few neighbours still living in the street from the old days did recognise us and told us everyone had moved except her and a white neighbour who lived next to Mr and Mrs Overhead. New migrants from Daman and Diu (the old Portuguese colony from India) who had migrated with European passports before Brexit were living in the areas we had once occupied.

I used to collect little imitation diamonds in tins. I do not know how that started but it was one of my preoccupations in the absence of toys. It must have been something we all did as young girls, or I did, and Shanti followed. She would copy me and sometimes it would irritate me, but we were close, and I forgave her. Shanti had a problem with her heart and was frail but had a lovely huge smile and exceptionally large eyes. I looked out for her at school and in the early days of frosty winters and snow. I remember that on occasion I would rub her feet and try to cheer her up as she wept because of the cold. We were both skinny at that age but somehow, I was the stronger and more resilient one of the two of us, and more her protector. She always looked fragile, and her parents quite liked me supporting her, so allowed me to come in and out of their home. Shanti rarely came to my place because our house was dingier and never as welcoming. I remember her house as always brighter, whilst ours was dark inside, rarely getting any sun. A door down from Shanti's house was a large house which we all envied. It is now a nursing home but for a time in late sixties it belonged to a member of the band 'Shawaddywaddy'. We used to hang around to catch sight of the stars.

Before his major illness, Dad was quite a frightening man and did not try to win children over with smiles or small talk. In fact, although my Dad was never physically violent in any way, and I cannot remember ever being physically chastised, he could frighten us all with his look. So naturally other children did not like to come to our house. However, the regular visitors on Saturdays were my Padmamasi (Mum's sister) and her children. They were our other closest relatives alongside Chaganbapa's family including Balwantbahi and his sister Bhaniben, who had six children and had become a widow while pregnant with her sixth child. Her eldest son was two months younger than me, and we had been in Kenya at the same time, and they joined us in Leicester a few years after we moved. She still lives in the house two streets away from Balwantbhai and his family.

Chandra, Tara and Suresh. Watching television was still a very important pastime and this photo shows the TV is on (possibly 'Z cars') and the stick-on top of the set is helping in some way (the aerial). I remember us fiddling with it.

Dahyamasa, (Padmamasi's husband) and my Dad (also called Dahya) did not get on well as there had been a falling out when Padmamasi came to England to get married - another match my Ajima had secured while we were in India. My Dad had to organise the wedding before we arrived in England and the budget was tight, but my Masa insisted on a Brahman priest to conduct the ceremony, or that is the story I heard. My Dad would not agree. It was in the days of weddings in front rooms and making do. It caused a rift between the two Dahya's. My Masa was a combative figure himself, so it was not a happy relationship between the men. However, despite this, I remember my Dad helping me get food ready to take to my Padmamasi when Shashi (their baby daughter) was delivered at home. Even though I was a child, I was sent to help with washing clothes and cooking over several days while Masi recovered from childbirth. Sadly, Padmamasi died in late 2024 and at her funeral my cousin Shashi recalled those Saturday visits when her Dad would go to the pub and Padmamasi would come to visit us with her son Naren and Shashi. The children feared my Dad and just played and chatted with us while the two sisters caught up with the news from India. I had not seen my cousins for years, but Masi's funeral reminded us of our childhood, and we laughed amongst the sadness as we shared stories and memories about those Saturdays in Wingfield Street.

I was only two months older than my friend Shanti, so we were in the same year group at the Infant School and then went to Mellor Junior School together. Shanti and I used to go to the Saturday morning children's film show at the Coliseum Cinema which was just round the corner from our house. It was a lovely Art Deco style building and quite lavish for a neighbourhood cinema. It was huge and through my research I found out it had seating capacity for 1,552 with 1,000 in the stalls and 552 in the circle and the proscenium was 35 feet wide.

By the time we started to frequent it on Saturday mornings, the cinema was floundering, but they were still showing Westerns and Hollywood films. For us, there were American cartoons to watch, like Bugs Bunny and Top Cat, but it got us out of the house and was a treat. It must have been cheap for us to be able to attend. I am sure my brothers and Shanti's brothers came too in the early days. Later, the Bollywood films were screened in the afternoon and there would be a real scrum to get in, everyone who had been looking forward to their film fix at the weekend. Later the Bollywood showings were extended to Sunday afternoons. When the Cinema declined, I remember Dianna Dors came to open it as a bingo hall. Later it was turned into retail outlets and a conference hall, banqueting and a wedding venue, but nowadays it looks sad and vacant, although the Art Deco on the outside still looks impressive.

For our community at that time there was nothing else - the Bollywood films offered the only entertainment beyond the new television programmes, still in their infancy and in black and white. In the Midlands, the BBC Pebble Mill studio based in Birmingham was the first to introduce a radio programme for new Asian immigrants called 'Apna he Ghar Samajiye' in the mid-1960s. I always thought it was an interesting title. Was it really suggesting we 'make ourselves at home in England' or was it inviting us to make ourselves at home? In 1968, the Asian programme called 'Naya Zindagi and Naya Jeevan' (New Life and New Living) arrived on BBC TV - a magazine programme for our community, presented in Hindi and Urdu on a Sunday morning. There were about four different presenters. I remember it so well especially the presenter Mahendra Kaur. It is something the whole family watched together, a bit like Saturday afternoon wrestling watched by all our Indian families. Recently, Samir Ahmed (a journalist and presenter on Channel 4) spoke on BBC Radio 4 Desert Island Discs about her mother taking her to the studios as a child, as she was also a presenter on Naya Zindagi and Naya Jeevan. I do recall a woman presenter, and it is amazing to think her daughter got to go to a TV studio during the era in which we were growing up. By the time I left home and graduated around 1977 there was an Asian Women's magazine programme called Gharbar. Later, these programmes merged into 'Asian Magazine' in the 1980's and continued to air on Sunday mornings till about the mid-1980s.

In our early days of arrival there was goodwill across the Asian communities of all religious backgrounds - Hindus, Muslim, and Sikhs. That was our experience. In fact, we all relied on each other and supported each other because there were so few of us. Usually, the places for worship were in our homes. Later the temples, gurdwaras and mosques began to take shape in converted halls and churches. In Leicester the Hindu community opened the Shree Sanatan Mandir in 1970 and this became the place we all attended for festivals, weddings, and prayers. Once the East African Asians came to Leicester around 1972 (although many came later having been dispersed in various parts of the country), the landscape of the city changed dramatically. But in those days religious prayers, bhajan mandals (devotional music and songs), and occasions like weddings also happened in small rooms in terraced houses. Families and friends would help prepare food for wedding parties and this continued well into the 1970s and early 1980's. In most religious communities the use of the home for weddings started to die down. Once there was a consolidation of different religious groups and castes, and the population from distinct groups started to grow, they had their own community centres or religious buildings in which wedding parties or ceremonies would take place.

By the late 1970s and early 1980s, I recall events when certain ceremonies and food preparations took place in the home, then the actual wedding day ceremony and food for wedding party was in the community hall. I loved the pre-wedding rituals of making puris and pakoras, and frying papad on a wok. The bride or the groom would have turmeric paste rubbed all over the body in a ritual to purify their body and make the skin look bright, a practice known as pithi before the day of the wedding. At my brother Suresh's wedding, we did all that at home (penno), then took our wedding party on a coach to the bride's hometown of Walsall where we had the wedding at the temple and community hall.

In time, caterers started taking commissions for wedding parties. Now, especially in Leicester and other cities with a sizeable Asian population, the wedding industry providing clothes, venues, catering, planning, hair and beauty and the humble henna painting, has become a multi-million-pound business. I had left Leicester in 1974 by which time this industry started to take off as did groups providing services to certain sections of the Gujarati community. This development was supported by the business and entrepreneurial acumen and activities of the East African Asians.

In 1975, the Shree Prajapati Association in Leicester was established, driven by the generation that came in the 1950's and 1960's, and helped by those arriving in the 1970's. Our community was growing and needed a physical base. The building, purchased in 1992, was large and cavernous and in a timber yard. It is now a sought-after venue for gatherings, Navratri and Diwali festivals and community activities for all generations. It is the go-to place for wedding and hall hire. It is a registered charity and there are similar other community places by different caste and religious groups in Leicester.

However, in early 1964 there was still only a small community from India and Pakistan. My Dad had a Sikh friend who had married a white woman. He had two daughters with her but also had a wife and children in India. I always felt sorry for her even in those days because I did not understand what she got out of the relationship. They used to visit us on Sundays and have tea. They were the first 'mixed race' couple with 'mixed race' daughters I had met. We are more likely to talk in terms of dual heritage now but generally the derogatory term 'half-caste' was used by nearly all the people. Neither community took the wife and her daughters seriously. I felt white women in these relationships were slighted by both sides. They were seen as oddities by both white and the Asian communities because they had crossed the boundary of 'acceptable behaviour' and married outside the norm. It was unusual, and my recollection was that white women in these situations were ostracised. Years later, my nephew (himself Indian/English heritage) was to play a lead character in a stage play, which was then made into a film, called 'East is East' (1999). The screenplay was by Ayub Din Khan, who had based it on his own experience of growing up in a dual Pakistani / English family in 1970s Bradford. The film won a BAFTA for the best film and was an important contribution to the history not just of the South Asians but of the complexity of the cross-cultural unions of the time. It reminded me of that family we knew, and although billed as a comedy it was poignant and sad to watch because of the racism and domestic violence it depicted, and the white women characters who seemed trapped in a strange position amongst all cultures and societies.

There were successful cross-cultural unions and evidence of them exist in literature, particularly in the middle classes from 1920 onwards but I did not come across them or know about them at the time. 'Asian Britain' – A Photographic History' by Sushiela Nasta published in 2013 refers to this issue. It is a brilliant pictorial history showing a rich South Asian presence and their contributions in Britain across class structures. There is a photographic reference to the young cast of 'East is East' as well as other artistic contributions from the South Asians.

'Mixed' marriages between Gujarati and other caste groups and the white population are more accepted now especially amongst educated groups but tensions persist in families and communities across the diaspora. The implications for us as a family around marriages across race and culture I will explore later.

Back to the period around 1964, we were also very friendly with a Muslim family. Again, they used to visit us and we them - I would say we were close friends. Ayshamasi was the mother of the family, and I used to play with their daughter Zubaida in the recreation park on Cossington Road. The 'Recky' as we called it, was the place Zubaida and I used to go on the swings… high! So high that I fell off and was taken to hospital in an ambulance. Luckily, no bones were broken. It is strange but I can still picture us, both standing on the high swings with long chains and working the swing so it would go higher and higher. That and pleasure from playing with skipping ropes and chasing about playing 'tag' was our main pastime. Later, the family moved to the Highfields area as more of the Muslim community lived there and the houses were older and larger for extended families. People of different faiths were beginning to move near each other. I remember going to their son's wedding and eating amazing food but cannot recall what happened to Zubaida. No doubt she got married and had children, but as we got older our lives were not so carefree, and it was not as easy to just wander off and play at the 'recky'.

Puberty was just an awful time for girls like us. We lost control of how our bodies were growing and taking shape. At the same time, we became a focus for the community as a potential wife for their sons and a domestic servant for the household. In my case, I felt so oppressed by not looking like a Bollywood actor and no one seemed at all concerned about my academic abilities throughout these times. The perception of beauty in a young girl was to be fair skinned, slim and with refined features. I did not fulfil these criteria. My brothers were often cruel; in the ways older brothers can be as children. Mum was hopeless at that time in preparing me for this stage of my life. Once you started menstruating and physically changing shape, our lives as young girls became more oppressed and controlled. For example, my job was making chai and offering drinks to guests but once I started menstruating Mum would not allow me to serve my brothers' friends in case I made 'eye contact'. And yet the pressure to function as an adult in terms of cooking and cleaning was immense. The situation was vastly different for the boys. There seemed to be no expectations of them in the home. I have forgiven Mum for humiliating me in front of her friends just as I started my periods, because I suspect she just did not know how to address this part of my development. She herself had undergone all that, just as she was getting married. I suspect she was just very frightened that I was developing and associated it with getting me ready for marriage. This was what my Mum was preparing me for, and in her world that meant pressure to start looking for a suitor. She felt even more urgency to get me to conform, and look and behave in a way that would make me ready for a suitable match. It was the stuff of Jane Austen but without the class snobbery.

Early education

In 1960s Leicester there was no special help for children who did not speak English, and we were meant to learn for ourselves. Our English was rudimentary, but our Prajapati community began to set up supplementary schools as our population grew. It was run by key educated people who could teach the basics of the English language and mathematics and built on the basics of our first language, Gujarati. These classes were all run by volunteers and took place for three hours on Friday nights (one hour per subject) and three hours on Saturday mornings. It took place locally in our junior school with children drawn from the Belgrave area.

In the early days of school, our lack of English made it exceedingly difficult, but my brothers and I were all bright academically, and that showed once our English improved. I was a bit younger so maybe found learning English the easiest, and our Indian school's focus on English grammar helped us. We did not have any other extra tuition, although my cousin Balwantbhai made us work through the 'red book,' called the 'English Teacher.' It was a big book bound with red cloth covering. It had a thick spine, but that bit of the spine covering had come away with wear and tear so just had plain buff paper exposed. It was a second-hand book in any case but was a brilliant introduction to the basics of English and grammar. My cousin worked for a shoe factory where they used brown paper with tar sandwiched in the middle. It was used for industrial strength packaging, not ideal as a writing paper, but needs must and there was never any spare money for frivolities like writing paper. He used to bring us a small roll from work for us to write on, and he would set us exercises and tests at the end of each chapter dedicated to aspects of grammar and syntax from the English Teacher. His English is not that brilliant even now, so it was good he made us do it. We looked up to him, as our 'older brother.'

In our culture, a nephew or niece of either parent was known as 'cousin-brother' or 'cousin-sister' to differentiate from hundreds of other 'cousins' who were distant relations; or even just people from your village whose parents we called aunt or uncle, so their children became cousins. The cousin-brother-sister titles gave them rightly the importance of close blood ties and we treated them as our siblings. I used to worry so much about not remembering the specific type of relationship and terms used for each, and often thought the generic cousin, aunt, uncle used by white families was preferable. It seemed so much easier than our overly complicated system. Now I am glad we have it as it is easy to work out which side of the family we are related to (see Glossary for relationship terms).

Once I learnt English I was reading avidly, and the free library was our salvation. The library in Cossington Street in Leicester is still there, right opposite the public baths, where we went to have baths and where we learnt the basics of swimming with school lessons, and by the recreational park, where we spent all our free time playing. These three services in our neighbourhood provided by the City Council helped us to live a much more meaningful life and let us grow physically and intellectually in our early days in Leicester. It makes me so sad that successive governments are stripping these essential public services from the lives of ordinary people. These fundamental public services are a bedrock of a civil society and benefitted us, as they should everyone.

My brothers were less interested in novels I recall, although we all went to the library to borrow books for our school lessons. At school we all started to excel in other subjects once we had a basic command of English.

Dad, like all migrants, wanted us children to achieve academically and not waste the free education on offer. But it was a gendered approach. My brothers were expected to do well academically, but as a mere girl, I was expected to do enough to get a job in an office (in the early days a hosiery factory may have been my parents' ambition for me if any).

I remember a door-to-door white salesperson coming round with an Encyclopaedia as he was no doubt targeting immigrant homes, recognising our parents' aspirations for their children's education. I remember the salesperson coming into our house and really selling the virtues of his product and how it would help us to progress quickly. Dad did want us to get ahead at school, but I think he must have agreed to the free index which was offered first before they hooked one into buying the volumes in instalments. My brothers tell me we only had the index, so I suspect my Dad was not seduced by the sales patter or more likely, he just could not afford it. We do not remember the index being that useful to any of us, but it was hanging about for a long time according to Suresh's recollection.

I left the infant school by summer of 1963 and started at Mellor Junior in the September with Shanti. Suresh started secondary school that year and Chandra would still have been at Mellor for another year or so before joining my eldest brother. We all continued with the supplementary schools for a couple of years, although I cannot remember when we stopped going. As in any Indian education setting it was a disciplined place and very focussed. I am sure all parents had to contribute to the cost of running it, but I reckon it gave better value than tutors in those days. The concept of supplementary schools continued with successive migrants where English is a second or third language, but it is a resource now provided by the local authority where schools have a higher concentration of non-English speaking children. I am sure with new waves of global migration and the needs of asylum seekers and refugees that the supplementary school idea still functions accompanied by private tutors. In my Gujarati community private tutors undoubtedly featured widely but we never had that experience.

Once all the lodgers had gone in 1966, I had my own room, and I loved it as I could read happily on my own. My brothers shared a room until they left home to go to university. Having my own room meant I could read late, even though Dad would shout at me to go to bed. Dad had found an office door he got from a second-hand shop for that room, and it had a frosted window on the top half, so he could see when the light was on. My room was basic with a lino floor, no heating and a small window that looked over the next-door factory walls - but it was my room, so I loved it and could read to my heart's content, frequently late into the night, despite the frosted office door giving me away with light shining through.

I tried to give my room a bit of a delicate touch, attempting a four-poster style by draping a sari. It was a cold stark room otherwise. By secondary school, I was reading avidly and began to discover Dickens. Great Expectations, Oliver Twist and David Copperfield were amongst the first books I read and loved. Later I moved on to Thackeray and Jane Austen, Emily Bronte and later books like Harper Lee's 'To Kill a Mockingbird', which is still one of my favourites. Many of the authors and books that influenced me came at secondary school. I began reading about inspirational women like Florence Nightingale who had been a social reformer and a nurse during the Crimean War, Angela Davis an American civil rights activist and Maya Angelo whose autobiography *'I know why the caged bird sings'* was to have a profound impact on me. It was to help me think that other routes were possible for women besides marriage. In the meantime, it gave me enormous comfort as a young girl, and I felt like Roal Dahl's Matilda - but without her powers. It was just magical having a room of my own and reading and escaping to other worlds or finding kindred spirits in the characters in the stories.

Before then, Mellor Junior was good for me although I can recall outrageous incidents with teachers. The head teacher was a middle-aged man called Mr White, and I always remember the morning assemblies when he would sing with such gusto. He was a short stubby figure with white hair, and I can still picture him, so animated, in those morning gatherings. I used to love singing the hymns and especially the Christmas carols. I know more hymns than any Hindu religious songs or bhajans. It was great to start to the day with the hymns even though the sermons that went with them were difficult for me to comprehend. There was a climate of increasing hostility and racism in Leicester, with more Asian migrants entering the city and with escalating racist behaviours by the white population. Teachers were not immune from the prejudice of the wider society and not that enlightened as a collective profession at the time. It is a vast generalisation but that is how it felt to us. They could get away with being nasty and there was no recourse to complain especially as our parents could not defend us even if they wanted to. Most of us children would have assumed that we had to just get on with it, recognising our parents belief that the education system was the route for us making it in England.

There was a particular teacher at Mellor, who had served a period in the army based in India. He was a hangover of a typical colonial who continued to misuse his power and position. He would take the Indian boys 'under his wing' and talk to them in Hindi and behave as if he were their overlord. He might have been helpful too, but he was on a power trip, creating a little 'Raj' in the school. I do not think anything sinister happened but reflecting on it I realise that by today's standard it seems unprofessional, particularly as the Indian boys were very deferential to him and he seemed enjoy his special role as the one who 'understood' the immigrants.

Chandra told me of a terrible incident that happened later at his secondary school. It was not unusual in the 1960's and early 1970's, so we did not even discuss it at the time. He told me this years later, when we were recalling our school days, and I wanted to include it in a lecture I was to deliver to students at Sheffield Hallam University. I was a lecturer at Bristol University in the late 1980's and 1990's, and I focussed a lot on racism in the criminal justice system, having been a probation officer during the riots and rebellions in inner city Bristol in the early 1980s. I was talking about total misuse of power by people in authority and this was a good example. Chandra's Head Teacher was a severe woman and used her power against defenceless boys in her school. There had been an incident when a window had accidently been broken. Without any evidence, she decided one of the Asian boys had been responsible. When no one came forward, as punishment she caned all the Indian boys, having decided that they were all complicit by their ethnicity. I think Chandra may have escaped the cane – saved by the school bell at the end of a break

I believe. Later, when he did very well in his O-levels by getting equivalent to A* grades in nearly all his subjects, this head teacher snubbed him, and Chandra said he felt crushed. She had already shown her racist attitude so it is easy to imagine she would take away any sense of achievement from my brother.

However, I do remember one exceedingly kind teacher in my first year; her name was Mrs Fox, and she was Dutch. She took our class to her flat in the posh end of Leicester – around Clarendon Park. It was beautiful. She had laid out a spread of sandwiches, cakes, crisps, and drinks. We were all astonished because no matter if you were an Indian or a white working-class child, not one of us had been anywhere as nice or had a spread which seemed so perfect. No one at the school had ever been this kind to us, and I really loved the fact that she put herself out for us working-class kids who were that early generation of the new 'multiracial' Britain. It was not a term coined till much later but on reflection that is how I saw it. She was a notable example of what a good teacher should be. I am sure if we gathered that class now, we would all remember that magical teatime in Mrs Fox's flat. She also brought a cat into class, and we would feed this on a rota. I used to hate the smell of canned food but loved stroking and feeding the cat. Mrs Fox used to wear kitten-heeled shoes and changed into flat ones in the class. I remember trying them on and loving the sound of those heels on wooden floors when it was my turn to feed the cat, and I was alone in the room. She was a petite woman and had small shoes, so they were perfect for me. It was in those moments that I wished I had been born in a white family, not realising that being white was only part of it – being white and middle class was the best and possibly having a white mother like Mrs Fox would be the ideal! That is when I must have had my first thoughts about being born into the wrong family and in the wrong culture, sex, and class. These are the issues I would learn to confront later in my journey and learn to love who I was. This included my identity, my gender, my politics, my family and community, my sense of service and a need to empower others. But individual teachers such as Mrs Fox provided early example of kindness, empowerment, and positive role modelling.

Mellor was also where I first met Sue. I got to know her because I became a 'late monitor.' This may have been my first experience of a position of power. Sue was a striking, pale-skinned ginger-haired girl. As brown, dark-haired people, we were a bit in awe of very fair skin and the colour of white people's hair and eyes. We did not seem to have the variety or shades of hair colour and were fascinated by blonde and ginger hair, and blue and green eyes that some white people possessed. At school, Sue was always late, and I should have reported her in my little book as a late attender - I think three 'lates' led to something like a detention, but she always had an excuse, and I never reported her lates. Our school was full of working-class children, but Sue was from more of a lower middle-class family background and seemed more privileged than most in our school. She was smart, confident, and ambitious even as a 9-year-old. She passed her 11+ examinations and went to a grammar school where I was to meet up with her again in the 6th form.

Food and shops

I cannot remember much about the Mellor days except enjoying school and learning. After a school day we would go home, and my brothers and I had to get part of the dinner ready. We had a basic mung bean sak on the Monday and most weekdays it was a frugal meal with basic sak and rotlis. There were Indian grocery shops around by this time and although there wasn't much choice we would go to Newington Road to a family shop and get what we wanted in terms of flour, rice, dahls and vegetables. On a Monday after school, I would put mung beans on to boil, and it would be ready for my Mum to do the vagaar, or tarka as now popularly termed whereby hot oil will have seeds popped and introduced into any dahls to effectively seal the flavour. She would also add spices when she was home from work before doing the vagaar as I was not confident at that age to get the balance right with the spices. I was also making rotlis by this time with a little help from my brothers. Chandra would help get the atta (flour) together with hot water in the bowl and do that bit watching TV and making the dough. We would take the dough and make little balls. Then I would go in the kitchen, stand on a little step and roll it out, and Suresh would help cook it on the stove. So, by the time Mum and Dad were home, we would have the dinner ready. Our family and community members would say what good children we were, but we were trained to help quite early in life as Mum worked hard in the factory and Dad worked in the evenings on his sewing machine.

Our food was basically a peasant type of diet. On a Friday, Dad would sometimes buy goods at the Leicester market, as it had a thriving fish and vegetable market. He would spend ages looking behind the counters and observing where the fresh tomatoes were, because in those days, traders would hide soft tomatoes at the back of the display, and back at home you realised they had slipped in a few squidgy ones. The stallholders would shout 'don't touch' so shopping was an intimidating experience. As for fish we did not have fresh cod or sole, only oily fish, like herring, mackerel and sometimes just fish heads.

On Friday, the Muslim man with a van would pull up outside our house and my heart would sink. The door on the white van would open and then pull shut and the man would walk down the side 'entry' and I would hear a rattle of the latch on the back gate and then clank as the door shut. I could make out the squawking of the terrified chicken and then no sound as the man slit its throat. I do not think I ever actually watched a chicken killed but on occasion I watched the man out of our window and saw him bent over the drain cover doing the deed. He would just leave it there - I assume money changed hands somewhere but cannot recall how. My job was to bring that chicken into the kitchen. I am not sure why this was my job as it is the kind of macho job my brothers could have been tasked with – maybe when I wasn't around, they did, but it was usually me. The recollection of those times was always of it being cold and miserable and I would leave the little coal fire in our main room and go out into the cold with a plastic basin to collect it. Because part of this task was also to clean up the mess left outside, through experience of doing this job every week I worked out that the sooner I brought in the dead bird with the hanging head into the kitchen the better. The longer it was lying outside, the more the blood in the drain congealed in the cold and then it took much longer to clean up around the drain. To be fair, the mess was contained in the drain cover, but in the days of no central heating it was easier to boil the kettle and there would be enough hot water to scoop around the drain and get rid of the blood whilst it was still fresh. The only drawback was that undertaking the task so quickly, after the man had done the act of halal killing, was that the chicken was still warm when I had to hold its feet and put it in the basin. I hated the whole thing but was quite pragmatic when it came to eating it.

My Mum did the demanding work of plucking, skinning and jointing the chicken to make the sak - better known as murghi noo sak - to be eaten at the weekend with hot rotlis. She would save the liver and the yellow yolk of would-be eggs. She would wash the liver, add a bit of salt, grill it, and share it amongst us three children. We used to love it; the egg yolks she would just fry in a little ghee or butter and if we were lucky, we would share that, or she would save it for my Dad as a treat to have with his little bottle of beer. It is strange how I remember the details of these little luxuries from that time of scarcity.

In India, we had chicken once a year, killing the chicken which had laid eggs for us throughout the year. It was an annual treat which became a weekly one in England. The chicken sak symbolised one of the first changes to our diet in Britain. Although poor by British standards of the time, our diet was already richer than the peasant diet we had in India. I think for me the ritual of preparing and making the sak weekly instead of yearly, showed we had made it to England. But the rest of the week we ate basic pulses like moong beans, potato sak, dahl, fish heads or fish scraps all with rotli and rice with the very watery toovar dahl. All this we bought from the grocers in Newington Street; we were their loyal customers for years before more shops opened and began to compete.

There were also the Joshis' who owned a small corner shop next to the Coliseum Cinema and there we would buy bread, sweets and tinned products as well as newspapers. They were our nearest go-to shop for general groceries. Nowadays, that shop is selling farsan and various Indian street foods, run by an old neighbour. Her children and grandchildren work there round the corner from our old house. In the Belgrave and Melton Road area where we grew up, there is an amazing array of shops and services which provide food and employment for the Asian communities across the city and beyond. We can buy any food including papad, pickles and snacks and savouries we had to bring with us when we migrated to England. In fact, accessibility to fresh, savoury and sweet street food in Leicester is the envy of all of us who do not live there.

One of the men from those days is the multi-millionaire who used to go from house to house to sell saris in a suitcase. His family were one of the first to open a sari shop, Milans, in the Highfields area in 1964, to provide saris and clothes to new migrants from India and Pakistan. He later moved to Belgrave Road amongst the old classic British firms like John Cheadle, Woolworths, Fine Fare and Wilkinson (later Wilko). The old engineering companies were also along this part of the Belgrave area as well as other manufacturing factories. The older retail shops were gradually replaced over the next 10-20 years, and it became a thriving shopping area, including service-based shops such as dry cleaners and a laundrette run by Asian families for the needs of the Asian community. Now that area is the 'Golden Mile' and as the name implies has a fair selection of sari and gold jewellery shops and outlets.

Dad's stroke

In my last year at Mellor Junior School, when I was spending lots of time with Shanti, Dad had a stroke. Our lives were then consumed by my Dad's health and him becoming totally disabled. The impact was devastating. We grew up very quickly in the summer of 1966. We were mini adults even before Dad's illness but left our childhood behind that summer and adapted to a new reality. We suddenly had to live on benefits as Dad lost his job and Mum had to give up her factory work to look after Dad full time.

His stroke was severe, a total paralysis of his right side, that happened at bedtime that June evening. The three of us were watching TV, and Mum went upstairs. She shouted at us and said something had happened to Dad. I remember we rushed to their front upstairs bedroom and found my Dad just not responding. Mum was extremely distressed, and we called the doctor. Our GP came and told us that nothing could be done for him that night. Knowing now that fast response is critical after a stroke, I wonder if he would have fared better nowadays or with a more sympathetic doctor.

Dad's face looked fine at the time and when he wanted to go to the toilet Mum tried to help and he fell. She felt his dead weight. That is when my Mum realised it was something serious and got my cousin over from their house. It was not until the next morning that the ambulance took Dad to a district hospital as they were sure they could not do anything for him. By then, his face looked dropped on one side, as is the case with strokes.

Dad was in hospital for about 12 days, and his boss came to see him; Dad recognised him and got very emotional. He started to use the term Ma (mother) from that day. It was a general term he called us all by including my Mum. His right side was paralysed from the stroke so he could not walk, talk, use his right arm or hands. All that the doctors could offer at the hospital was physiotherapy and no speech therapy as no one could speak Gujarati. They said that in time he could improve but the prognosis was poor for any real recovery in speech and movement. It was the most devastating experience for all of us and after a total of two weeks in hospital they suggested he could stay in a nursing home as Mum was working, and we were so young. Mum said she would not leave him in a nursing home and decided to give up work in the factory, and in today's terminology, she became his full-time carer. Mum was aged thirty-one with three children aged nine, eleven and thirteen, with no income. We were to live on state benefits for six years. At an early age I began to navigate the world of welfare benefits as they related to school.

July 1966 was the year England won the World Cup and there was excitement everywhere. We can only remember our lives taking a turn none of us had foreseen. The rest of the country were euphoric with England's success. Unfortunately, that success has eluded the England football men's team since then. However women's football has really developed since then, and the England women's team won the finals at Euro 22 - a spectacular achievement.

Dad came home, and Mum did everything for him initially. Our community had not witnessed anyone who had become so disabled in a flash. My cousin tried to give us practical help in negotiating the welfare system. 'The community' were unfortunately, at times, more of a hindrance than help. In fact, people would come to pay their respects, but many just wanted to see what had happened to him and give their verdict on the whys and wherefores. I used to hate the constant flow of people coming and going and I had to make chai for everyone visiting. Making chai is not simply putting on a kettle and sticking a teabag in a mug. It necessitated making chai from scratch with tea leaves, sugar, milk, and masala, including washing up the saucepan, cups and saucers in between visitors. It was relentless in the early days of Dad's stroke, as we were dealing with the emotional impact and the practical difficulties alongside being respectful to whoever happened to pop by. I now think why did we put up with it? Why did I comply with that constant stream of making chai? The answer is simply I had to. It was what was expected of me, and, in those days, it was accepted that anyone who comes to your home gets an offer of tea at the very least. It was our cultural response, but as a girl in the family my role was to serve even if I was emotionally distressed. We got all sorts of people visiting and there was no gatekeeping or screening-out of unkind visitors, who were more voyeurs than helpful friends. Poor Dad became a bit of a spectacle on display and regularly got annoyed. On reflection, we would not allow that behaviour nowadays. I suppose it might have allowed Mum to exorcise all her grief with the repeated recounting of the story and crying. It was an extraordinary time, those early days of his stroke.

In time he started to walk with a stick, once the physio department got callipers fitted on his right leg and attached to his shoe. In the 1960s there were statuettes of little boys and girls with callipers on, attached to a collecting box for the 'Spastics' Society'. Dad was an adult so I used to look at these statues and often wondered if our family could benefit from these funds or was it just for the children. I became quite into welfare rights, recognising that there could be resources to help families like ours. Dad used to cry regularly as he felt so diminished by his inability to talk and converse. I remember the medics and professionals would say 'he had lost his power of speech.' It is a phrase that stayed in my mind. Why didn't they just say, 'he is unable to speak any more'? It was my early recollection of professional language that was meant to differentiate the lay person from the way professionals speak - something I would later in life go on to challenge in my work and advocate 'patient public involvement' in the health service, and research in health and social care. This was a significant focus for twenty-five years with the National

Institute for Health Research (NIHR) and charitable organisations such as the Cancer Alliance, NHS cancer networks, and public/patient involvement.

Not being able to speak and communicate is so devastating when it happens suddenly. It is difficult to know if he had lost part of his memory, but undoubtedly he could remember things as time went on and much of his memory came back before it was all gone again with the second stroke six years later. I used to pray that a miracle would happen, and we would wake up and Dad would be well again. I was quite into the power of prayer at the time, in the absence of anything else. Even as children, by then we were intermediaries for our parents with the NHS and any officials, as we would help translate. Our cousin did help with official forms but on day-to-day things we were the official translators and interpreters. I have spent many years working on strategies in the health system in Bristol to get adequate standards of interpreting and to get professional recognition for the role of interpreters. Innovative technology has helped and places with a larger non-English-speaking population may have better developed operational systems, but I suspect many children still function as their family's interpreters in health, social care, housing and official settings.

Dad was collected on the transport provided and taken to day centre twice a week where he had physio exercises (including flexing his fingers and writing with his right hand) and activities making things. He made a wooden fruit bowl that I kept for years but later lost with my various moves. He would try to sew with a piece of fabric, needle, and thread and say in his broken language: "I will sew again one day". On other days when he was not at the day centre, he exercised on the floor and with adapted aids to help move his arms and legs in our living room. He undertook these exercises daily without fail and was determined he would improve.

In his pre-stroke days, he had made a beautiful suit for himself in light grey fabric and in all our family portraits or formal photographs such as Balwantbhai's wedding, he is wearing it. He was a good tailor and prided himself on producing high quality work. My parents had about one good year when we were not living in overcrowded conditions and had the house to ourselves. Dad had his treadle Singer sewing machine in the front room which was known as the 'sitting room' and had been our family lodger's bedroom. Dad would always bring a box of his work home, so each item of his work had a value depending on the time and skill needed to complete. He was often doing alterations and helping put parts of a bespoke suit together in the evenings after a day at the workplace. Employers clearly exploited him, some who had been migrants from Europe. The situation for newer migrants is not that different today in Leicester where migrants are often exploited by some who had been migrants before them. This has been shown by the exposure of the conditions and pay of workers in hosiery trade especially operating from small workshops in Leicester during the Covid pandemic in 2022.

Looking at Dad's logbook he was on average earning £7 per week, but by working long hours (84 plus) he could earn about £12 12s per week or £13 16s. It really depended on the type of work he would be allocated. In the tailor's logbook he had to record his work for his bosses and there is coding against each piece of work, with the hours and pay attached to that piece of work. It was very variable in terms of rates per job. They all seem extremely low pay for the hours worked.

An example of a tailors log, showing pay for piecework before June 1966

One of my lasting memories is of Dad at the old Singer sewing machine, and Mum sitting by him helping with buttonholes or hand stitching. Dad drank little alcohol, and Mum was always grateful that he was not a big drinker as her own father had had a major problem. Dad's drinking was very restrained. He would open a small bottle of 'Double Diamond' and share the content with Mum, carefully pouring out the beer in two small glasses. It was moderation and something they did only occasionally. It was their time – when they would talk and mull over their plans for us and themselves. Despite a hard life in those early days in Leicester, these moments when Mum was sitting helping Dad and both chatting were in retrospect very precious. I wish I had had a camera back then and captured those images. They had only a small window of this kind of 'contentment' in their married lives. He prided himself on doing 'clean' work and not working in a factory or foundries as other people of our community were – although their earnings were better because the jobs were hard but unionised. But Dad's poor health meant he was better suited to tailoring and bringing work home meant he could earn more by spreading his workload. Unfortunately, this short episode of what I remember as a 'good time' for my parents did not last long and was a fleeting phase of fond memory for me.

Living with Dad's disability

Dad's stroke had a catastrophic effect on our family, hampering our ability to earn money and move forward. Mum spent her early years in a new country looking after Dad and us. He had his daily exercise regime in the morning which he did in our living room and at lunchtime ate two rotlis and a bit of sak, never anymore. As we did not have a proper bathroom, my Mum would bring a glass of water, and he would swill out his mouth in a plastic basin as one side of the mouth would need help to clear because he had little movement. He was meticulous even with his problems. I write this just to show the level of care Mum gave him. In the afternoon, he would try to practice writing or undertake activities and exercises given to him by the day centre. Mum would shave him in the morning, and he would always look smart in his ironed pyjamas. He stayed dignified, looking clean and respectable, helped by my Mum's care and attention to his needs. When he attended the day centre in the early days he cried as he did not want to go. In time, he would just do his best to enjoy the creativity on offer and recognised it got him out the house. His old exercise books show the efforts he made to write words and draw with his paralysed hand. He veered between thinking he would get better, and all would be fine, to feeling bereft by his disabilities which were overwhelming. It was hard not to feel sad watching him crumble from a man who had gravitas in our community to a man who was at the mercy of people around him. We were all very respectful of Dad because we had grown up in a culture that had at its central core: respect your parents. We cannot imagine ever being disrespectful to him.

I suppose one of the greatest indignities was he had a commode which we needed as our toilet was outside, and it was hard for him to sit there. Mum dealt with that side of things, but on occasion when she had to go out, I had to help. He tried to tell me he did not like me to help and would get upset. I was still quite young, and I found toileting particularly distressing. It was one thing that put me off ever going into nursing, which I had considered as a career. But it was hard for my Dad when I did have to help him and on occasion he would cry at the indignity, as he perceived it. As a parent he felt it is not something children should have to deal with at any age. He appreciated what we did for him and that became clear in his attitude to us.

Later, when I was about 13-14 and in the throes of adolescence, I used to have shouting sessions with my Mum over housework. I felt so oppressed and misunderstood. I thought other people must have life so easy. As I stormed up to my room one time, Dad called me softly from downstairs and although he could not say my name, he used to call me 'Bhanki' (the name of his niece). He tried to say, 'Do not worry, things will blow over. Let us have a cup of chai.' He could not articulate it, but he spoke to me very gently. I did genuinely feel he understood that I got the brunt of my Mum's wrath when things were stressful for her. He was observing things, and I really think at times he was reaching out to me in a way I never imagined he could. He was certainly a softer person with Mum and became a kinder man. Ill health and disability do change people in quite dramatic ways – sometimes maybe it promotes humility in a way other things just do not.

Occasionally he would get annoyed with us when he considered we were treating him like a child or being patronising. Every day as part of his ritual he would go for a walk. Mum would change him into his smart trousers, shirt, coat and a hat and his stick. He had callipers attached to his right shoe, so he was able to walk independently with them and a stick. He had a circular route, but Mum always sent my brothers to follow him in case anything happened. She would get on with the cooking and I would help with mashing spices in a large pestle and mortar and then help Mum with making the rotlis while Dad was out on his walk. On one occasion when my brother Chandra was working hard on his A-Level revision, he had to follow Dad and as usual he would hang back, so Dad did not get annoyed. He must have been looking at a bike shop on Melton Road and when he looked up to continue and follow Dad, he could not see him. Dad had got on the bus to the Highfield area where my Mum's Jagukaka (our Ajabapa's brother and the one my Dad lent the £20 to all those years ago) lived. To their complete surprise he arrived at their house. Meanwhile, we were all beside ourselves. Chandra was tearful, Mum fretting and all of us scouting the neighbourhood. Eventually, Jagubapa (to us) and his son turned up with Dad, and we realised that he had just wanted to exercise some autonomy. He felt good that he had out-witted Chandra and all of us. It was a difficult scenario as we did not know how Dad could truly cope independently as he could not communicate with the outside world.

We were never sure how much of his memory was affected by the stroke. Often his frustration with the life he had lost manifested in tears or pure annoyance. On one occasion he spent hours trying to gesticulate and illustrate on paper something he really fancied eating, and it was something we just could not put our finger on; in the end the penny dropped, and we realised he wanted jalebi - a yellow batter fried in thin spaghetti-type circles, then dipped in sweet syrup. We are not a sweet-eating family, so it was hard to even orientate ourselves to this kind of food. In those days, even in Leicester getting fresh jalebis was hard and he lost the desire by the time we realised what he wanted.

Dad was always a dapper dresser and liked quality in all things. He had brown leather shoes, which he could not wear anymore, and Chandra tried to wear them. Dad got angry, maybe because they were his, a bit like his watch that he was obsessed with. On reflection thinking about it now, I realise that he had hopes of getting better and being able to wear them one day. He was possessive of his things, and my brother wanting his shoes must have felt like losing control of his few worldly possessions - like losing hope for a normal future where he could wear them again. Chandra was hurt by Dad's reaction and it seemed a waste as they were just gathering dust. Quite rightly, he could have worn them as we just did not have money for quality things. Years later when we were going through some things, we came across his watch, which again he had been very possessive about. It was sad that it was then of no value as it wasn't working and was hardly worth repairing as watches had become so much cheaper to buy new. Chandra's daughters bought their father an Apple watch recently, and when he was talking about how good he found it, I did smile thinking about Dad's old watch.

Secondary school

The September after my Dad's stroke I went to my secondary school. My brothers were at a new comprehensive, co-educational school (mixed sex), and my secondary modern was a girl's school. My brothers' school was newly built so had good facilities. There had been efforts to send the boys to the same school, but I do not think anyone bothered to work out if my school would be good enough for me. I guess the fact that it was a 'girls school' was another positive thing for our family as segregation of the sexes was important, especially in context of the girl's education. I don't think we knew about the 11+ examination and Suresh really wouldn't have had enough English in the first year to be able to manage this, and Chandra had only been in England less than two years before the 11+, so neither could have passed without more help in English from the schools; something which is more possible in multiracial schools now, I hope. I had longer to get to grips with English, but we never had sympathetic teachers to tell us how to progress, so we were not aware of critical exams. I am sure I would have passed the 11+. At the time I would have taken it, my English had improved dramatically, and a little guidance and support may have done the trick. I say this with certainty as when I started at secondary school I was transferred onto the top stream within weeks, and I came top of the class in my end of year exams in all subjects including English. Interestingly, my brothers had also been transferred to the top stream in a similar way on arrival at their co-educational school. In another time and place our academic abilities could have been recognised earlier, and our education journeys would have been less of a challenge.

There were four streamed classes in my first year of secondary school. As I moved to the top set, I was the only Indian child in the class although there were many of us in the lower set. I had forgotten about it all but was reminded of that time as Suresh found my old school reports from that year in his loft. Considering the circumstances at home with Dad and truly little encouragement from the family, I was doing very well but I did not really get any praise at home. I think all three of us just got on and recognised we had to do our best. When I see young migrant children, especially refugee and asylum seekers, I do feel that there is a thirst to use the education system as a base to build a better life, and that helps if academically it is possible to do. Not everyone can achieve in this education system without help, so support and direction towards skill-based careers is so critical for future employment for those who prefer other routes to academic ones.

I found out that being on benefits we should get free school meals and free school uniforms, so after talking to our deputy head about our personal circumstances I negotiated that for our family. It was preparation for my career to follow in social work. However, despite my academic ability, I did feel the hand of racism descend in the year I had to choose my O-level and CSE subjects. For a start, our school was so badly resourced that we had general sciences and not split sciences as in my brothers' school. My teachers put me in for CSE in some subjects and I was told not to worry and that if I got grade 1 at CSE then it was equivalent to O-level. I was so upset that I was put in for CSE in English. That was my favourite subject, and I worked hard on my weekly essays, and I knew I was good enough to get a decent result. Chandra came to parents evening to represent my interest in the absence of our parents being able to do it. He is only two years older than me, and I guess the teachers, with their insensitivity about my parents' lack of availability, would not have taken him seriously. They would not reverse their decision on the O-level/CSE issue in English. I was really upset but I found out that I could register with an exam board outside the school – in other words 'do it yourself' without the help of teachers to work on the curriculum. In the end, I did that and got my English O-level plus a clutch of others from the school and CSE's in practical subjects. In CSE Needlework I made a snakeskin, jersey material mini dress, in the 1960s style with collar, long sleeves with cuffs and criss-cross string front using eyelets. I wore that dress so much and it was my pride and joy as I felt chic in it. I am not sure I can make anything like that now.

In one of those mixed ability lessons after lunch, I was sitting with Shanti, and we were all sewing away. Shanti let out a burp quite unconsciously – she was a slight figure so maybe it attracted the attention of the teacher as she was near us. The teacher peered over her glasses at Shanti and with all the anger and fury she could muster, started to shout and verbally abuse her for being 'so disgraceful.' I will never forget her saying to Shanti: "We think that kind of behaviour is extremely ill mannered. You people think it is acceptable to behave in that way". We all just smirked because it was quite funny, but the teacher's anger was out of order and disproportionate to the 'crime'. I really wanted to go and shout back at her, and I still recall how impotent we all felt. Shanti had affronted the teacher by her 'lack of manners', a concept lost on us at that time as we would not have seen this as bad manners. We would all learn the social and cultural mores of our new country… in time. Luckily, Shanti did not get the ruler, because she looked so tiny they were probably worried it would backfire on them.

In the summer of our early secondary education, Shanti had a heart operation. I would visit her often during her convalescence at hospital and home. It subsumed most of that summer supporting and comforting her. I was a good friend to Shanti throughout her school life and her parents always knew I looked out for her. As with all friendships it was a two-way thing and outside of the school day and during the holidays we spent time together whilst at secondary school. We went to Indian functions and dressed up for Navratri, Diwali and weddings in our saris.

Tara and Shanti with our saris c. 1972. The Colosseum can be seen at the end of the street

Sometimes we went to see Bollywood films and talked about our future and about boys. We experimented with make-up and hair, and enjoyed shopping when we got the chance. She went on to have reasonable health after the operation. We drifted apart once I left for university. Later she got married and had two daughters. In her early 50's she had a brain haemorrhage, after a slight knock on her head. She was on blood thinners, and this had caused the haemorrhage. The family contacted me in Bristol, so I hurried to her hospital bed and said my goodbyes to my dear friend. At the funeral I could see that she had had a very full life with family, colleagues at work and friends and was pleased she had shared our joint childhood stories with her husband, who recounted them as we sat with her on her hospital bed.

I remember 'getting the ruler' for talking in class on occasions, but physical abuse from my teachers was thankfully just that for me, and not as bad as stories I heard from the Indian boys at the other schools. Smacking, caning and 'chastisement' for school children was a common thing and no one really bothered to tell their parents even if one 'got the cane.' At my secondary school, apart from Shanti, I was very friendly with Lesley who I knew at Mellor as well. She was a white girl from our neighbourhood, and her family were Christians. They treated me well in the days when school friends' families, especially white ones, were not that welcoming. As Shanti was in a different stream to me, I made a range of white friends in my stream. I got into the hockey team and played every Saturday in all weathers.

The whole gender-ridden wider society had low academic expectations of the girls but extremely high ones for the boys. This was particularly so in our community although it became more enlightened later with the Asians arriving from East Africa. They were much more liberal in aspiration for their daughters. Capitalist intentions may have driven them, but they were keen to support the girls in academic achievements as well as the boys. I was always in the top three of my class at secondary school, and I could see I was doing better academically than many of my peers. I enjoyed what the school had to offer so would use any opportunity afforded to me. It was a shame my secondary modern school had so few resources and little ambition to exploit my talents and those of my classmates. I took part in county sports as well as the school hockey team, supported by a teacher who encouraged me and found me a spare pair of hockey boots. I became a house captain for the 'Blue House' so got to wear a blue sash which gave me huge pride. Of course, there were the usual Head Girls and Prefects, but I never succeeded in being one of those. There was an Indian girl who

I was very jealous of called Sunita. She was a prefect and had sleek hair and looked perfect. By the time I reached 13-14 I was changing shape and appearance as all young girls do hitting puberty, except Sunita who continued to look perfect. I started getting spots and filling out. I had so much hair – long and thick but was not allowed to cut it so I had huge plaits or a ponytail. Increasingly, I hated being in the house and felt the criticisms around my looks were relentless. Much of this on reflection is because my Mum just did not understand what happens in puberty. She herself had been married off incredibly young so she equated menstruation and puberty with preparing me for marriage and unfortunately the whole focus in those days was on how you looked and if you could do housework – two important attributes for being a desirable young woman.

Despite all the shortcomings of my mediocre school it was a respite from the burdens of domestic drudgery at home. Dad's disability meant Mum's life was hard and she would get irritated by me as I was not the conforming daughter she had envisaged. My brothers were her salvation, and I was a burden – or so it seemed to me at the time. Consequently, I would take part in anything that I could outside of the home, and when I had to be indoors, I was doing domestic chores then escaping to my room to read. I often felt emotionally crushed. I was and am a headstrong person and am so glad I was. It saved me from accepting so little from myself - although it was also the reason Mum found me difficult. In the Indian family context at the time, the girls had to be compliant and not have views and opinions. This was more so having migrated to England where families were protective against western influences on the girls - being challenging or outspoken equated to a western trait that was abhorred.

I worked out that I had to conform to some extent, and I was in that way strategic - so I did cook and clean the house, especially the kitchen on Sundays, and even cleaned my brothers' bedrooms. On Sunday after lunch, I would clean the cooker, wash dishes, clean and mop the floor. Sometimes I went to Pramila's house, an Indian friend who was not a rebel, but I liked her quiet acceptance of life. We would make small cakes, made from early packet mix called Viota. They were small fairy cakes with green and red angelica on top. The box of mix would yield about a dozen cakes, and it was my earliest experience of using ready mix and enjoying it. It is sad that I remember this detail, but it was a treat of sorts to do something different from what was the mundane part of my life in those years. I made fish pie and rock cakes, and things at home from scratch because our cookery classes (later called home economics and now food technology) were surprisingly good practical lessons, and I did learn how to cook 'English' food. We could do with those sorts of practical lessons in school now as they were thorough in teaching the basics. I loved my wicker panier basket we needed for cookery, laden with ingredients with a clean tea towel over it, then getting back home having cooked something nice that was not sak and rotlis for a change. All my family loved the food I made as it was of a good standard. I still have the Good Housekeeping cookery book I bought for less than £1, which is now falling to bits. I enjoyed both needlework and cookery as they added a dimension to life that had practical applications. These classes were held in mixed ability classes, so I got to be with my Indian friends.

I enjoyed the music appreciation classes which gave me a very basic grounding in western classical music. We listened to this, but we were not offered an opportunity to play any musical instruments in school. The library classes allowed us to explore books. The teacher taking that class was a published author of romantic historical novels. She would read us chapters from her book, which I really enjoyed. Our parents were not able to read to us so the teacher reading aloud was the next best thing.

We did not go on formal holidays but, again referring to my earlier writing in Part 1, we would have a lot to do with Mum's cousins in Coventry. Shantimasi (the daughter of my Ajima's brother in Navsari) and her husband, Norotammasa, were good to us. We used to go during school holidays to visit them and after Dad was ill, they would invite us to stay to give us all a break. They had a daughter, Gita, and a son Narendra, who were similar ages to us, and we really enjoyed being with them. My Masa was a bus conductor, and a very warm and generous man. Amongst other things, we visited Coventry Cathedral on numerous occasions with him. Unfortunately, Masa and Masi have died now, but we remember those early days with great fondness. They gave us and Mum those moments of respite and provided the nearest thing to a holiday break. I hope Naren and

Gita know how important they and their parents were to us during those years.

Dad's final days and after

I turned fifteen in December 1970 and Dad had a second stroke in mid-January of 1971. He had worked so hard to get better and this was just the last straw. He moved to a nursing home called Zachary Merton. For days Mum visited, but he lost so much weight he was effectively starving because he could not eat anything. I am not sure there was much of an attempt to feed him, and it was their version of an 'end of life' plan without being explicit. We were told he was receiving no active treatment but when I saw my Dad he had a hollowed-out face with sunken eyes, and when Mum lifted the blankets, his legs looked like two sticks. It was a picture reminiscent of the starving people that we saw on the television news at that time. It was shocking to see, and that image stays in my mind forever. I realised for the first time at that moment that he was dying. I guess Dad had also given up hope although it's hard to know how much he was aware. He died on 4th February, a few weeks after the second stroke. After all the years of hope and hard work, my Dad's death felt so unfair and futile.

I remember that day clearly. I was waiting in the dinner queue at school when our neighbour's son came to fetch me. I do not think I even told the teacher that I was going home but I knew instinctively my Dad had died. As was the tradition in those days, people from my community started to come round as the message spread, and the women from our family would cook basic sak with pulses and rotlis and feed us while my Mum and relatives wailed and cried. This went on for days. At Dad's funeral the coffin came, and the religious ceremony was conducted, which included putting yogurt in his mouth. Yogurt has quite a significance in religious Hindu rituals. He looked like someone else. He was laid out in his suit, but his shirt was so big around his neck as he was so tiny by the time he died. I wish they had not done the ceremony as he would have hated stuff around his mouth. Dad was always so neat and tidy and the last image I had of him was a messy face with red tikka on his forehead from the religious blessings. There were so many daffodils around as we went for the cheapest option in winter. Our street being so small was full of our relatives and members of our community. Dad's funeral was one of the first in our Prajapati community, so everyone turned up. The women did not go to the crematorium in those days. I cried for Dad, but even during this period of sadness there was little time for private grief. I decided to undertake weekly fasting on Thursdays for six months so his atma (soul) would be at peace. My Mum did something similar. People in my community still do fasts on a Thursday for all sorts of reasons, but I never really understood why it was a Thursday. I think for me it just helped focus my mind on my loss.

Mum widowed at 37 and from that day she did not wear any adornments except her two gold bangles

We all went back to school soon after the funeral. My Dad's death left a huge vacuum in our lives, and without fail I have remembered the day he died on the 4th of February every year – and always buy a bunch of daffodils. Eventually Mum went back to work and got a job at a hosiery factory. I started work as a Saturday girl at Fine Fare supermarket on Melton Road. It was good to earn a bit of money and be able to buy my own clothes and make up. It was a great liberation as none of the children in our community ever had any pocket money given to us at that time. It was the preserve of white families. The Saturday pay was not great, but it gave me my first taste of economic freedom. It was also my first experience of racism in the workplace. My manager was a middle-aged man who was kind and considerate. He knew I worked well so respected me for that. A few of the women who were cashiers and shelf-fillers (and that is what I did mainly) were quite annoying and one was particularly spiteful. She used to sing the Simon & Garfunkel song 'Slow down you move too fast. You got to make the morning last'… but the way she sang it to me was really to say I was slow and lazy which I guess was her way of using a racist trope. I was only fifteen and more likely to get upset than dismiss it for what it was. I was able to work on the deli counter sometimes, and I loved doing that until a white woman told me not to serve her meat with my dirty hands. I was upset and went to the toilet and cried. My manager waited outside and told me not to let ignorant people get to me. In those days you can count that as a supportive gesture, as he reassured me that I was a good worker, and he was incredibly pleased to have me working in his store. Those odd moments of prejudice and racism were not that unusual in Leicester of early 1970s and we just absorbed and managed it. Such a personal racist verbal attack in the workplace was however a new experience for me. I later went to work at British Home Stores and a DIY shop in the High Street. I cannot remember dealing with personal racist attacks in those stores. Managing raw food seemed to encourage a racist outcry from some customers who deemed brown hands as dirty.

With the combination of puberty, hormones and the growth spurt that followed and the community becoming aware of me because of my dad's death and the funeral, I began to attract attention from them as a potential young wife for the eligible and not-so-eligible males from the Prajapati community.

I was a 'silent feminist' in those days, in that I read and watched things on TV and discussed women's rights with some of my teachers. One of the things that really had an impact was watching the series 'Shoulder to Shoulder' about the Suffragettes. It starred Sian Phillips as Emmeline and Angela Down as Sylvia Pankhurst. I can remember buying the magazine that accompanied the series. I was also greatly influenced by the early TV dramas. Play for Today was a great series for highlighting social issues and made us all more aware of the class politics in Britain. Watching the early works of Ken Loach like 'Kes' and 'Cathy Come Home', and other plays like 'Edna the Inebriate Woman' with Patricia Hayes were groundbreaking and so important for my political awakening. The late 1960s also had the kitchen sink dramas and films like 'Saturday Night and Sunday Morning'. Even though my life had none of the freedom some of the characters had, I still would empathise with the pregnant woman trying to have an abortion in the film 'Alfie'…just identifying with people with no control over their lives, and usually they were poor women and families. I was also going to lectures and meetings in the Highfield area which might have been put on by the Indian Workers Party. I did not really understand who they were, but the lectures were interesting and led me to join CARD (Campaign Against Racist Discrimination) because I thought I wanted to be involved in struggles against racism even though I was not always clear about their political leanings. I did get a sense that Black people and Asian people were in a similar situation in fighting against racism. I was educating myself more broadly than school and home would allow. The whole Civil Rights Movement, which was covered on TV had a major impact on me and I very clearly saw myself in comradeship and solidarity with other people and communities who were discriminated against in the UK and the USA. Also, the right-wing in the form of the National Front was on the rise in Leicester at that time so I was searching for some common bond with 'coloured people' from different backgrounds and began to understand the political definition of the term 'Black' very early on in my journey. Later I would go on to be an activist in Bristol in areas such as the Pro-Choice campaigns for Women's Right to Choose and following on from The Civil Rights in America I was heavily involved in the Anti-Apartheid Movement including supporting boycott of goods and services to and from South Africa.

People started asking if I was of marriageable age and whilst my Mum said I was still young, she told possible suitors and their families to 'see and observe' me whilst I was at Fine Fare working at the supermarket – she was thinking ahead. Often, I did not even know this was happening but sometimes I guessed, and so for me this was the ticking time-bomb of an arranged marriage. I kept thinking how I could stall this process until I was at least eighteen by staying on to do A-levels. I do not think I dared to even think I could go to university at that point. When I think of that period now, I wonder how I stayed at all sane. I always felt my family were seeing me too superficially, but even with accumulation of all the forces at work, including racism, misogyny, and painful objectification of me as I went through adolescence, I somehow managed to keep hope. Part of this was because I believed their horizons were too narrow and limited, and although it was at times so painful, I felt good that I could raise myself above this. I did possess a certain amount of self-determination and self-belief. I knew I had to be resilient, and that has helped me throughout my life. Years later, when I left home and was recognised for my attributes, including being seen as 'ahead of my time, enthusiastic, passionate, principled, and courageous' by colleagues and friends, I did feel vindicated. In time, many of my family (especially my Mum) and community would see me like this, so it was reassuring.

About six months after my Dad died, my first act of rebellion was getting my hair cut. I went to a salon near the Town Hall. As a young woman there are so many images of how one should look, and the pressure for young women like me to fit the perfect Indian feminine profile was as oppressive then as it is now. Girls in my community were expected to keep their hair long and as I did have exceptionally long, thick black hair there was a greater pressure to preserve this 'gift'. Despite my growth spurt, enabled by the onset of puberty, I was destined to be short in stature, as was the case for all of us in our family. Having thick black hair that went past my backside meant I looked even shorter, and my hair did not feel like an asset, but a hindrance. Also, psychologically I associated long hair with women's subservience, and the covering of hair for women as a sign of respect to men always made me unhappy and cross. Women in my family regularly had to cover their hair with their sari in the presence of their husband or older male relatives.

At that age, like other girls I also wanted to be fashionable and was experimenting with clothes and styles as much as possible. I wanted the opportunity to have a cut that would show off my hair and help me be more fashionable. Mum agreed for me to get it cut, even though she knew all my relatives would disapprove. I had promised that it would be 'an acceptable' length and my brother took photos of my hair before the cut.

Tara's hair. Taken just before it was cut for the first time

I offered to be a model so did not have to pay for the cut. I had a just-above-shoulder length bob so not too short, but less than half the length that it had been. The hairdresser put it in a ponytail and cut the length first so I could keep the hair. Then they styled it a little bit. Mum kept that ponytail for at least thirty years before I encouraged her to discard it.

I think she did agree that my hair was a burden, as she herself had long thick hair but had it in a bun all her life. It was the first time my Mum understood my needs and wants because she could see that my demands were only a normal part of me growing up. It was our first act of defiance against the immediate family and community expectations. My cousin Balwantbhai was shocked when he saw my hair shorter. Once I left home, I went on to have short bobs, and spiky punky hair over the years. I have been able to use hairstyles which express my personality and have not had long hair now for years – except for a while in my twenties when I did grow it and enjoyed it, but that was my choice. My daughters on the other hand love their hair in longer styles and hate their hair short.

After Dad died my Sunday afternoons followed a pattern. After the ritual cleaning which followed lunch, I would work on my English essay while watching Sunday matinees. It was an enjoyable time that I had to myself as Mum would try to drag me to a wedding or the temple, but I hated both so she would go off. My brothers were often out. The Sunday matinees on the TV were great as I had the house to myself and sometimes my essays suffered as I tried to squeeze the essay in having run out of time in the afternoon. That is when I would stay up late finishing things I had not done earlier in the weekend. Escaping the home whenever I could led me to take part in outside activities. I joined the St John Ambulance Brigade as a cadet with Lesley, well before Dad died. That was great fun learning first-aid and getting badges for extra activity and duties at various events that needed first aiders. It got me out the house every Wednesday evening and allowed me to make friends and socialise. I was less involved with other Indian girls but from time to time was invited to join garbas and dandiya ras (folk dances) which we would perform at events such as Diwali. I joined but I did not play a lead role in this kind of activity – I was more of a follower because of my ambivalence.

It was near the end of the secondary school that I began to really feel that I did not want what a lot of Indian girls in my school wanted. Their parents and my Mum wished for the same things: an arranged marriage to a nice boy with good family, and for the daughter to have enough English on leaving school, with just enough education to get an office job or job in the bank as a clerk – anything more might lead to higher ambition that would lure you away from the domestic bliss promised. There were working-class white girls in my school, and some did well academically, but no one I knew in my year went to the Grammar School to do A-levels. It was the end of compulsory education year and most went to work. I know a few got office jobs and some went to work for hosiery and textile factories or in retail. That was more to do with the limited ambition of the school than the ability of the students. The 11+ and its early segregation led that generation of white working-class children to feel less valued and created a real class division if they did not go to the grammar school. Within Asian families it was more a gender divide, in that boys were encouraged to do well no matter what type of educational system they were in.

My friend Lesley married a young Polish man when she was seventeen. I was in the sixth form by then and just could not understand why she would want to tie herself down when she did not have to. I went to her wedding in the church and then the reception in the church hall. I often wonder what happened to her as our paths diverged and we lost touch. Her family were not well-off and were practicing Christians. I was always grateful to them as they did involve me in their family events. I also attended Sunday School with her – again it was good to get out of the house, sing songs, learn about Jesus and take part in activities. For a time, I am sure I wanted to be a nun romanticising religion; watching films with Ingrid Bergman had a lot to do with that idea. For me, the church outings were always a treat. One of these was a day trip to Alton Towers and Skegness with the Sunday School. Lesley and I had fallen out on that occasion, so to some extent that trip was marred, even as Elvis was in the charts singing 'The Wonder of You' at the fun fare. I would not pull out of going on the trip and miss a treat to go on a church outing.

We had been to Alton Towers with my family in the past. Balwantbhai took us in the days when my Dad was ill. Outings with the Indian family were always hard back then because of the open hostility and racism we attracted in public places. Firstly, there would be a crowd of us so that drew unwanted attention. Balwantbhai took a carload of us, and I sat in the boot so it must have been an estate car. We would have stood out in any case. In those days, before it developed into a theme park, Alton Towers was a delightful place for the gardens and basic rides. We spread our colourful rajai (rugs) amongst the carpet beds of formal floral displays. Out would come the bhajias and parathas and dry spicy potato sak. Nowadays our food is acceptable and even admired by people. But in the 1960's and early 1970's it was 'smelly and foreign'. Sitting in places where we would be conspicuous was not ideal, and I often hoped the earth would swallow me up. It was always the kind of attention many of us young Asians hated but somehow the generation above us could not understand why we were embarrassed.

It was a process many of us young people went through (shame and embarrassment of being different) but in time it made some of us stronger and resilient, and some of us went on to challenge racism and embrace cultural differences and promote anti-racism and anti-discriminatory policies and practices in our work and activism.

I certainly did this in all my professional work which followed, including professional social work with a focus on anti-racism in social policy and the practice of social work. Later I continued with this focus in academia and in education, training, research, and publications. As teachers/facilitators of the Probation option on our Social Work course, we worked hard to address issues of institutional and systemic concerns and the impact on sentencing, particularly of young black men and women. As a social work team of educators and trainers and researchers addressing other options (children and families, mental health, community work and work with marginalised communities) we worked in partnership with many colleagues on the wider equality agenda with all sectors including the very dynamic voluntary sector.

Then after I left the University, I undertook consultancy work in research and evaluations in health and social care. On the NHS, as a Board member of various health trusts in Bristol for over twenty plus years, I led the work on equalities. I was the Chair of Bristol Race Equality in Health

Partnerships for over ten years, bringing together leaders and workers across statutory and voluntary and black-led organisations. It was an innovative and a creative partnership facilitated by some wonderful staff who have gone on to exciting leadership roles in Bristol and beyond. I was also a Board Member representing Bristol in a ten-year national programme called 'Race for Health' working with thirteen to fifteen Primary Care Trusts in the country to really focus on improving health for our diverse communities. It became a passion and commitment for me to address the wrongs in the society we grew up in. I worked hard to address the inequalities in our society, which at that time for me were around issues of 'race, class and gender.' However, it cost many of us dear as internalised racism, together with coming from a working-class background, had eroded our confidence and affected our self-esteem. As we pursued our careers, we had to unlearn the internal voice which would often try to 'keep us in our place'. Luckily, I was able to embrace my Black / Asian British identity as I began to develop self-worth and awareness.

This was achieved through political activism, reading widely and writing about it in an academic context and choosing careers that allowed for that exploration to be put into practice. There were years of debates, some often heated. I had many white friends and colleagues, and we worked alongside each other forming partnerships to address the wider inequalities in our society and particularly racism. In many settings I was the only non-white, visible minority presence. At various times my feminism was tested with what I termed cross-cutting issues of class and race with white women friends (often referred to as intersectionality in the current debates). But I recognised then that we had to build alliances wherever we could to work towards a more equal society.

In my professional role I was often ahead of the curve in addressing concerns around patriarchal structures and systems and undertook innovative work with women. I do believe the early days of challenging patriarchy in my family and community, and racism within society, together with living in working class areas with white and Asian poorer people in my neighbourhood provided the framework for my professional and personal life. We argued for separate spaces to support women and other black and brown people in respective organisations in the public sector – that led to an accusation of separatism by some colleagues. But these spaces of specific 'Black-led' groups were an important stage in the development and support for people who defined themselves as Black. The politics around the terminology of 'Black' to include Asian people has shifted dramatically in recent times. Certainly, I and others for over 30 plus years used the political definition Black to identify ourselves with the wider struggle against racism. The term of 'Black and Minority Ethnic' (BAME) was used for a time to encompass us all. Now 'people of colour' or 'Black and Brown' or Black and Asian are more accepted in public-facing discourses. As I write this a newer terminology is being adopted including Black and minoritised people reflecting the changing communities and evolution of the language.

Back to the early years of the 1970's, the atmosphere was febrile, and it was the height of racism with the National Front particularly active in Leicester. It was further aggravated by the resettlement of East African Asians in Britain. Leicester City Council had made a statement discouraging them from coming to Leicester, so this further inflamed race relations tensions in the city. I remember walking to school in the evening for a school show rehearsal, hiding my long plait in my coat because I feared white racists could cut it off. There were rumours going round that a girl had had her plait cut by young racists.

In between finishing O-Levels and starting my A-levels, I worked all holiday as a shift worker at Walkers Crisp Factory. I enjoyed packing crisps and trying to beat the clock to see how much I could do. I did not get a bonus as a temporary worker, but I enjoyed the challenge, and the day would go faster. I worked 6.00 am – 2.00 pm shifts. They had (and even more so have now) a big Asian workforce. At the time some of the Indian masis (the term used for all older Indian women meaning 'aunties', rather than their first name) would have problems with their payslips or other concerns and many of the women did not speak good English. They would ask me for help, and I was quite good at resolving their problems with the 'foreman or lady' as they were called in those days. There were of course many tensions between Asian women and white women in the workforce that I was witness to, including food consumed at lunch and the smell of curries and turmeric stains in the wash basins. I am pretty sure that if I was working there permanently I would have ended up being a shop steward. I enjoyed helping the masis and they teased me about joining them at Walkers, saying too much education would not help with eventually cooking dahl and rotlis for the family. They were not convinced my life would be very different from theirs in the end.

It was a good pay for me at the factory, and I went back again twice in successive summer holidays. It helped pay for all my clothes to go to university and my brothers also worked in their holidays in Jimson Wood factory, so we all put some money towards buying some furniture and carpets for Mum too.

Sixth-form and onwards

I started in the sixth form at Newarke Girls' School between Imperial Avenue and Fosse Road South in September 1972. It was a grammar school then, and saved a headache for Mum as it was, again, a single sex girls' school. I had to catch two buses from our house to Narborough Road. The school was impressive to look at, sitting proudly on a large field with cherry blossom trees lining both sides of a path from the front gate to the school entrance. We were in the 6th-form hut where we had our own cubicles to work, and we were allowed to put posters up. I really liked the feel of the place and oddly enough didn't feel out of place academically. It is now a community school. My friends from Bristol moved to the area with their son and had another son after moving; both sons attended this school and did very well academically. It is so strange as I drive past nowadays, as it looks the same as it did all those years ago. They have kept the old school front intact and added new buildings behind so is still an impressive building.

Here I met up again with Sue who I knew from Junior School. I also got very friendly with another Indian girl, Renu, and other white girls like Denise, Helen, Ros, Lyn, and Carol. Unfortunately, having gone to a secondary modern limited my choices in the subjects I could choose, so I enrolled for English, Biology and Geography A-levels and some extra O-levels. Renu's family were from East Africa and for me seeing them so nurturing of Renu's studies and ambition made me realise that I could at least get to university, and that the limitations placed on me by my family and by racism and classism within my secondary education could be overcome. I knew lots of other white working-class girls in my school who should have been encouraged to go on to higher education too. Having Renu as a friend was good for me as she was the first role model of a brown Indian girl who was bright and interesting being encouraged to do well and pursue a career by her family, rather than being prepared for domestic servitude. Ironically, I was devastated when her mother rang me to say Renu was expecting a baby after we were at the first year at university. It was not a planned pregnancy so a shock to the family. I heard that Renu left university to have her baby, but also that later she completed her degree and then taught maths. She married her partner who was Indian and from her caste, so her family supported her. I think it all worked out, but I was sad she did not stay in touch. I did not hear from her again although in the two years in the sixth form she was great fun, and her family provided an alternative role model to the one I was used to.

As well as Renu, I spent quite a lot of time with Sue. Again, a very different family scenario with a lower middle-class white family than I had met during my secondary school friendships. Sue was an only child, and her parents invited me over on a few successive Boxing Days for lunch and merriment. This was such a contrast to our house where Christmas was a normal day with just more television programmes as we did not celebrate the day. Sue's father worked for the Leicester Mercury in distribution, but I don't know if her mother went out to work. They were a welcoming family and liked her bringing me along to family occasions. Sue's uncles and aunts and cousins would all come to the Boxing Day gathering and play a variety of musical instruments and sing, play games and have a beautiful spread. At Sue's house I tasted smoked salmon for the first time. Sue was often featured in the Leicester Mercury for her achievements of one sort or another. I think my liaison with families like Renu and Sue, and other girls in the sixth form, helped to make me feel less isolated and began to expand my horizons.

Sue and I became good friends over those two years. After our A- Levels her parents bought her a second-hand car, and we went to Cornwall for a week as well as a cheap weekend away in Paris. We had an exciting time, and fun. It was my first time away from home. I did not know at Mellor Junior that she would later become an important person in my life between sixteen and eighteen, and someone in the background for many years into adulthood. In fact, she had a presence of sorts until I was in my early fifties. I kept in touch with her parents for some time via postcards and Christmas cards. We were in touch during the early days when I moved to work in Manchester before my social work training. I went to stay with her in Oxford when I was working as a qualified probation officer, and she visited me. But we did not see each other much after that except for Christmas cards contact. I got an invitation to her wedding but could not attend. Our relationship only ended after a lunch in a café in Oxford where I was attending a meeting, and we arranged to meet after about a 15-year gap. She told me at that last meeting that she was living in Scotland and still an academic. Her parents were moving to Scotland near her, so I was pleased to hear they were well and near their daughter. By the end of a coffee and sandwich in Oxford, although we enjoyed seeing each other, it was clear we had little left in common. The relationship had come to its natural conclusion and neither of us maintained further contact.

Out of all the subjects I took I loved English Literature the most. My teacher was great and an incredibly interesting and knowledgeable man. For the first time I went to the theatre with the school to see 'King Lear' which we were studying, and I enjoyed all the syllabuses. It is only years later when my eldest daughter was doing her GCSEs that I realised how the content of the syllabus has improved in terms of diversity from my experience, and I feel it was due to people like us in the public sector and wider campaigners in education, including progressive teachers, that those changes were achieved. Although in my time we would have benefitted from a different kind of a syllabus, with more ethnically diverse writers represented, I am pleased that I had some of the benefits of exploring classical literature.

My biology teacher was an older, white-haired woman who was a prickly character, and I think I would have done better in her class if she had not been so undermining to pupils like me. I wouldn't say she was bullying or racist – it was more that she looked down on the kids that had moved from secondary modern schools. We were not as sophisticated or as rounded – which was true as I barely understood the Latin names in botany having not studied Latin in my life. The grammar-school girls did two languages and Latin so in the sixth form just carried on building on their knowledge. I realised that in certain situations I just did not have some basic background. Having done general sciences meant that in biology I lacked knowledge that would have helped had I studied chemistry, which informs some aspects of biology. However, I did enjoy biology and did well in it. For geography I had two teachers. One was a classical grammar-school teacher and the other a younger, hippier teacher with a beard and longish hair. He was more contemporary and liberal in his values and approach. Near the end of term, he used to ask us questions like: 'how many of you want to influence the way our society works and develops?', or something obscure that I quite liked. I am sure I put my hand up as even then I did want to do some good and have some impact on people's life and I'm sure I wanted world peace!

I did other extra-curricular activities and again played in the school hockey team, continuing things I had done in my secondary school. I also did archery, played badminton and was good at table tennis. I may have also taken part in City sports; the details are a bit hazy, but I remember doing well at javelin at one of the city events. I took part in a school talent contest with my friends and remember playing Mr Higgins in Pygmalion. On reflection I was possibly quite bad as I had never seen the film 'My Fair Lady'. Ros (one of my friends) played Eliza and based her performance on the film, which impressed me a lot.

At a girls' school, sixth formers were not always very nice, especially at the end of year revues with the skits of teachers. Often, they were amusing but sometimes they would be tinged with innuendo around sexuality. I'm not sure I knew anything about sexuality, spending all my energy in fighting off arranged marriage 'tea ceremonies' at this time. I'm not aware that other girls discussed sexuality but the general influences of the 'Carry On' films and their deprecating humour of the 60's-70's was possibly the driving force behind the end of year reviews. It would be totally inappropriate now, but it also is a useful reminder of how bad the situation was for many people. It was only when I read the book and saw the film 'The Naked Civil Servant' based on an autobiography of Quentin Crisp, that I began to understand sexuality and the persecution of people who were not straight or heterosexual. Mocking teachers, even for end of term frivolities was always difficult for me from my Indian home background as it was ingrained in my culture that utmost respect should be shown to all older people and especially teachers who were seen as imparting knowledge and wisdom. The two years at this school was an exploration of how you could get a balance between respect and challenge, and yes, even have fun with authority figures.

David Bowie was doing his Ziggy Stardust tour, and the 'cool girls' in the sixth form were into bands like that, but my little group of friends were into The Osmonds. I liked David Bowie and T.Rex (I had a Mark Bolan poster in my bedroom wall) but was never allowed to see them in concert so could not be part of that group. Renu put on a dance sequence based on 'Crazy Horses' by the Osmonds and as I liked dancing, I joined them for the end of the term review. The Osmonds had been on a tour in UK in 1973 and there had been mass hysteria around Donny Osmond. On arrival of the tour at Heathrow Airport there had been an incident where the weight of fans had caused a roof to fall, resulting in some fans being hurt. The Osmonds were quite big in the day and were the forerunners of the boy bands to follow. There were about five of us girls who bought white flared jeans and put black sequins on the sides. We Indian girls were good at sewing on sequins as many of our families used to buy plain saris then trace intricate patterns on them onto which we, or our mum or auntie, delicately sewed on sequins. My Mum crotcheted a raffia border which was then pressed and sewn onto a green sari. I remember I wore it often. I digress, but my point is sewing sequins was something we grew up doing. Renu choreographed the song with our input, and we performed this at the talent show at the summer fayre at the end of term.

I was keen for Mum to see me perform. She was not good at attending any events but amazingly she did come with Shanti and her mother Dhaimasi, and they were really impressed by our show. I think it was the only time my Mum ever came to an activity that I was involved with at school, and she was surprised by the grandeur of the school and by my range of friends. Until then she had never been to my school. In many ways it was her own lack of confidence in speaking English that stopped her ever really taking an interest in wider things her children took part in, and that affected her lack of curiosity or interest in things outside her immediate experience at that time. It was not until much later that Mum would try to articulate in English with gestures and words and appreciate the world beyond her immediate sphere.

My brothers had both done well academically and gone to the sixth form at Gateway School to do science related subjects. Other Indian boys were attracted to science-based subjects too, so there were more of them at their school. Suresh got his A-Levels. Chandra continued to do well academically, despite having a very racist headteacher, certainly at the O-level stage. He seemed to have more friends and enjoy school and cope better. Overall, Chandra and I were probably more outspoken and gregarious as individuals. Around this time or a little earlier, my Mum's cousin (our Mama) a medical student came to stay with us from South Africa. Mama was a rather slick and confident man born into privilege and wealth. His mother was my Ajima's sister and had been a huge support to Ajima in India during the 'poor years' described in Part 1.

In South Africa, the system of apartheid affected this side of the family, who were designated as 'coloureds' under the regime. This meant they were subject to segregation as were all non-whites. So they sent their son to England for medical training. Mama must have stayed in hospital accommodation because he just came to eat with us and was, I felt, slightly arrogant – or maybe we translated his air of confidence as arrogance. He was fond of Mum but was not particularly sympathetic to our plight. This was when Dad was ill, and things were difficult. Mum would make him nice food like fish sak, and he would leave quite a lot of the food on his plate. I used to wash the dishes, so would get cross that he had no idea how hard it was for my Mum to make ends meet, and that his waste of food cost us money. However, he got praise from our community as he was going to be a doctor, and Chandra began to set his heart on achieving that dream for himself. He had told me he had planned to do economics or banking. However, the high status afforded to Mama being a medical student sealed Chandra's career choice, and to an extent Dad's illness had also functioned as a catalyst for him to consider medicine. Chandra liked a challenge and the prestige that went with being a professional, for children of poor migrants that was an important motivator in those days. He would face challenges in his career and experience some racism (in medicine) towards Asian doctors. I know he was rejected for a job he should have secured at a top London hospital because there were already several Asian doctors in the unit. Presumably they felt it may devalue the unit to have another Asian person, I think he even heard that explanation in his feedback. I am sure he had many other experiences like that one. But he went on to specialise in renal medicine and became a consultant. He worked in diverse areas such as Manchester, South Wales, Leicester, and Peterborough. On retirement his hospital in Peterborough named a building after him – the Dr Chandra Mistry Renal Unit – and we are immensely proud of his achievements and his contribution to the NHS.

Again, this standard of aiming high as Asians became the norm for the Kenyan Asians but in our families from rural India, it was a leap of ambition not usually associated with anyone from our immediate community. Suresh was expected to do well and had ambitions as the eldest son. He went to Salford University to do Electronic Engineering but after his first year came home. He was very bright and intelligent, but he suffered with bronchitis and asthma, and experienced some overt racism from teachers and peers that had a profound effect on him. He sometimes talks about teachers who ruined his life so there was a lot he faced without support. As I mentioned before, the impact of raw racism and of internalised racism on our generation is difficult to comprehend. It is hard for me to speculate what led a bright young person to walk away from university, although I know from my own experience at Aston University, that engineering courses (and technological universities) would not have been the most enlightened or liberal in those days. Suresh came home after his first year, but later successfully completed a City and Guilds course in London. He lived with our extended family in Wembley, staying there on weekdays and coming home at weekends. When he finished his course, he returned to Leicester and joined a company working in the TV department for many years. Later, he secured a post at De Montfort University supporting students with media and technology. Fortunately, his health and family life turned out well and he still works hard in the community doing charitable works in Leicester in his retirement.

As for me, after years of thinking my life would be submerged in a kind of marriage dystopia at the age of eighteen, I too managed to pass my A-Levels and was allowed to 'escape' to university in 1974. There were stipulations and conditions to leaving, such as I may not be allowed to finish the course if a suitable match came along.

I did not realise it then, but I was leaving home for good except for a brief period at home after graduating.

PART 3: Post 1974 and beyond

This covers the period of when Mum first went back to Desh (homeland), and me leaving home to go to university, then changing courses and institutions. Returning home briefly before moving for employment and training for Professional Social Work course. Employment as Probation Officer in Redditch and then Bristol.

Mum and family moving house and expansion of our families. Culture clashes and evolution to British Asian identity. Our multi-racial family, and a new generation of Indian and dual heritage children and grandchildren.

Buying my first house – symbolic and tangible act of independence. My significant first visit to India in 1984 (after our migration) with my friend Janet while Mum was there as a 'bridge' with my Indian family. The life-affirming impact of this trip. Marriage, family and changing career including political activism.

Managing tensions of family roles and relationships in a socio-political context and the changing world. Breakdown of 'traditional family' structures and Mum's move to independent living. Key challenges to adapt and acclimatise to the changing demands to her role, authority and health.

Transformation to British Asian citizens and a new frame of reference for our kutumb (extended family).

Our changing lives

Mum did travel to see her family in India, shortly after I went to Aston University in 1974 - the last member of the family to leave home. She seemed unworried by what I might get up to in Birmingham. In fact, within a brief time of her arriving in India, I was in Birmingham walking up to the 'Tavern in the Town' with some girls with whom I shared accommodation in an old convent in Saltley. The place was bleak, and I shared a room with a red-headed Irish student who I had only just met. I did not even drink in those days, but it got us out of the dismal place. As we walked to it, the pub was blown up by an IRA bomb attack. There were two pubs bombed that night in Birmingham. There was mayhem and I could not telephone Mum so rang Suresh. People died and many were badly hurt. My housemates and I were lucky we did not to get to the pub any earlier. I do not think Mum ever knew the scale of what had happened, and I don't think my brother ever really comprehended how near we all were to serious harm that night. The 'troubles' in Northern Ireland were at their height, with 'Bloody Sunday' having taken place in 1972, when 26 unarmed civilians were shot and half of these were killed by the British Army, leading to many bombings in mainland Britain.

It was a strange start to my independent student life and after all the close supervision at home I was suddenly 'let off the leash' with no scrutiny by any of the family members. Luckily after this incident the University did offer us a student flat in the student village in Handsworth. Most of us who were initially at the old convent were housed in a flat of six girls. It was much safer, and the village had all the amenities that we could want in our first year.

It was the first time since our migration that Mum was able to go back to her homeland, Desh – this time on a plane and not a ship or boat of any description. It was quite a restorative time, allowing her to reconnect with her family. I'm sure there was an element of relief for her to have got us through the school years with the hard life she had had since migrating. When my own daughters went off to university, I felt a similar sense of relief at having got them through the adolescent years. The whole issue of marriage for her own children was still a big theme for her visit however, and we know she spent money preparing for dowry and gifts attached to Suresh's and my probable marriages. Chandra was still completing his medical studies and went to India to do his placement as part of the course and then travelled on his own around parts of India. He did get to spend time with our Mum and the family too. My Laduma had died six months before my Dad, so none of us got to see her again. This is a great regret for Mum and all of us. But our Bhulima was still alive at Mum's first visit back home, so that was a huge bonus that they got to spend some time with her. There are photos of Mum that Chandra captured, showing my Mum happy in the company of Bhulima and Jiviphoi (my dad's sister) and a collection showing her in Munsad making chai, rotla and having quality time with Bhulima.

Mum, Jiviphoi, Bhulima c.1974

Mum with Bhulima in Munsad

These photos show Bhulima wearing her sari in a katchodo style. It is worn that way so women can work in the house and the field. Usually, these saris are cotton or voile fabric. Mum wears her sari long as many do nowadays and they can be a variety of fabrics. Each style has the palo at the front. When we lived in the village, they would gather vegetables and put it in their palo and tuck the end forming a pocket, so they could still have their hands free.

Mum making rotla in the back yard where there is also a water pump (dumki)

She spent time with her own mother, my Ajima, as my Ajabapa had become a missing person soon after my Dad's stroke in 1966, eight years previously. Ajabapa had a huge row after one of his drunken episodes which led him to walk out of the house and never return. Searches and investigations lasting years ensued; some showing sightings of him in strange places and towns but never coming to a positive conclusion. It took about 20 years after his disappearance for the family to accept that he might have taken his own life by jumping into the sacred River Ganga or maybe he became a sadhu. A sadhu is a religious seeker of spiritual enlightenment, uncluttered by material possessions or family entanglements. It was a difficult conclusion and never a satisfactory one for the family when there was no evidence of what might have happened to him. I know that my Ajima and my mamas did not have any sense of closure despite trying to track him down for many years. Ajima spent many years dressing as a married woman with a red tikka on her forehead but at some stage after a long time-lapse, she accepted that she may be a widow.

The time visiting and staying with our family in Munsad and Navsari was such a positive experience for Mum. It had been relentless, adapting to the cold climate (both emotionally and physically) in Britain. Then, with little time to adjust to a married life, she had to bring us up when my Dad was suddenly disabled. This had taken its toll. She had become a full-time 'carer' (not a term used at the time) at thirty-one and widow by the age of thirty-seven. Mum's world was very much her immediate family and friends in Leicester. Again, as with the case after return from Kenya to India, her self-confidence was so much greater than in Britain. Mum was always more herself in Navsari and Munsad and she loved the time she spent with both sets of our families and neighbourhood friends in India. For people like Mum who migrate it takes years to feel at home in the new land, especially when her emotional ties were still back in India. It would take a few more years for her to feel that England was a place she belonged, when she had a new generation of her own grandchildren and after her own mother died some years later. Her new expanding family and her roles with them would help her make an emotional attachment to Leicester and England as her natural home (but not yet).

After her first visit to Desh she returned from India after a couple of months in the bosom of her families. She bought a lot of things for mine and Suresh's potential marriages as she foresaw them coming in the next few years. I still have the silver jewellery for my bridal outfit and feel so guilty that she had used her savings. Even then, Mum knew I would not like gold, though it was considered a better investment for the future. On her return her priority was to find a suitable young woman for Suresh.

Higher education: new horizons and parallel lives

As I was at Aston University on a 4-year course I was warned by Mum that I may not be able to finish my degree as I would be 22 years old when I completed, and that was considered too old for marriage prospects. My course at Aston was Behavioural Sciences with specialisms in second year in subjects like Psychology. I realised I was more interested in Sociology and Social Sciences rather than Behavioural Studies. I also had to re-sit one of the exam papers, and this clarified for me that I should change course. I transferred to Kingston Polytechnic into the second year of their 3-year Social Sciences Degree course, saving me a year and moving to a course I would go on to enjoy. It meant that if I did have to have an arranged marriage, at least I would have a degree by 21 – a bargaining chip for future negotiation for marriage. It was the best decision I ever made, and I have sustained close friendships from those heady days living in Surbiton and Kingston. I missed Aston only for leaving my friend Doreen, the Irish friend I had shared a room with at the start of my student journey. We stayed in touch until about 1984, and now mainly through Christmas cards. I briefly met her in Belfast in recent times when we were visiting as a family. Our lives are very different now, but she was one of the few people who was into authentic curries in the days when others were generally hostile to the 'smells and garlic', and she came to stay at my house despite me warning her that our house had no indoor bathroom.

Ironically, despite my new Surbiton/Kingston setting (a white middle-class suburbia) I met and got to know more Asian friends and students than I ever did at Aston in 1974/5 (a multi-racial part of Birmingham even at that time). I met Indian women students experimenting with relationships with both Indian and white men, some deciding to go all the way and others hedging their bets and enjoying the freedom just to go out, without people judging. One of my friends I was in halls with, Manju, was going out with another Gujarati man and both were happy, well-suited, and in love. However, in the end he went back to Leicester to have an arranged marriage because they were not from the same caste. That would not happen now, I hope. I was later invited to her wedding to someone she and her family had found through their networks. He was a Gujarati and from her caste. She was a graduate in Economics and was 'a good catch'. She was very dark skinned and would not have been considered attractive by the standards of some in the Indian community. We used to discuss what was considered beautiful and attractive in our communities and helped each other to dispel some of the archaic myths that were perpetuated, not just by men but also by women in our families. I thought she was beautiful; she had a most incredible smile with an amazing bone structure and was reasonably tall. Some of us were struggling with our self-image as Asian women with brown skin in a white, often very racist society in Britain and then fighting prejudice from our own community over what nowadays would be termed 'colourism'. But we were happy to have each other to affirm that we were doing well, and there was a sense of camaraderie across South Asian and International student societies at Kingston that I had not experienced at Aston. We had social and cultural evenings, cooking and sharing wonderful food from different countries. I learnt to cook a decent biriyani at one of those occasions.

I had many Indian friends in Kingston. Rekha was a Gujarati 'Patel', from Wolverhampton. She was, to me, a 'very modern' Indian woman; she was studying Languages, Economics and Politics and spent a year in France and so spoke perfect French. She was a year older than me and after graduating went on to work for a large car manufacturing company in France. I admired her and she was in a long-term relationship with a white man. Years later when that relationship ended, she went back to Wolverhampton and got involved in the Gujarati society, and decided to live her life surrounded by all her family and friends within her Indian community. Her parents were very liberal and educated, and were instrumental in getting community education off the ground in their area.

They were also involved in the Gandhi's Home Rule Independence movement when younger and living in India.

Rekha decided to live in her 'Asian family' and be known as a successful businessperson, but within a structure where she was not trying to blend in. We were all trying to fit into the world of white people; in the end, she made an active choice not to. However, she maintained a broad friendship group across countries and cultures. To that extent she was a great internationalist and certainly very well-travelled. She actively chose to go for an arranged marriage at an older age and married a divorced businessperson from India who already had children. From what I could see she became a great daughter, sister, stepmum and masi to her nieces and nephews. She became friends with the husband's ex-wife who was a doctor who provided her with good advice when Rekha got ill with cancer. She seemed happy with her choices in life. Throughout her life she was seeking the perfect religion and found something that helped her to face an early death at sixty-five. I went to her funeral and marvelled that she had experimented with living different lives but in the end, she died amongst her close family, with Hinduism at her core and some of her friends, like me, with her French and other English friends, including her former white partner and his wife all there to say goodbye, as well as the whole community into whose bosom she had returned.

To me, Rekha is an example of a woman of my generation of Gujarati women who grew up in an era where we had to create our own path around identity and belonging, who as young pioneers went to higher education, didn't choose arranged marriage after school and didn't follow the traditional roles over time. But later in her life she made that choice on her own terms, including pursuing the religion of her family.

There were also a couple of Sikh women at Kingston, one on my course, Harbi and another studying Law, Kami. Kami was from a rich Southall family and great fun. She used to wear brilliant clothes and generously let us borrow them from time to time. Her family were quite strict, so she would go out for meals and flirt with men, but her approach was that her friendships were clearly defined, and a relationship with any man was only for flirting and enjoying platonic friendship.

For her 21st birthday her family put on an extravagant party for her in Southall to which we, her student friends, were invited. We predicted she would end up marrying a rich Sikh man from her community. I am sure she did, but we lost touch so it's hard to know. I would love to see how her life evolved because that was yet another model of how an Asian woman of my generation and a similar cultural context made a different kind of choice.

Harbi came from a liberal Sikh family. She had been on a kibbutz and seemed to have had opportunities that spelt liberalism and freedom. She had exceptionally long traditional wavy hair which she wore loose and looked a bit like Meena Kumari (the classical Indian actor hugely popular at the time). She was fair-skinned and would be considered beautiful by all our Indian communities. Harbi had a radical streak, and we shared similar politics. I ended up supporting her when she decided in our final year to live with a white student on our course. Despite what I had interpreted as a liberal family, they were devastated by her choice. Her much younger brother wrote her a letter saying, 'didi (sister) please come home'. I remember us weeping together as we read it. In the end, she did marry him. I understand the couple divorced few years later, but I'm sure Harbi's family were re-united at some point. We noticed in time that some parents who rejected their children for the choices they made in respect of marrying white partners or people outside the community were later allowed to re-join the fold, as more young people opted for a wider choice of partners. But at the time it was very distressing to have made the choice to break away; she was torn between her own needs and being cut off from the family she loved.

Going to Kingston certainly gave me opportunities to mix with Indian and South Asian students. Most of us led parallel lives straddling a more 'western' life at university with the traditional one back at home. For me going home to Leicester was also to fall into subservience because my Mum still had a noticeably clear demarcation of male and female roles, as did my brothers. I did not want to rock the boat too much, so I complied with the norms. It's hard now to believe how I became a chameleon, having a strong feminist beliefs and values in my student life whilst behaving in a subservient way back at home.

Studying social sciences, and particularly sociology, was bound to have an impact even though I was leaning leftward in my politics well before then. After all my leaving prize for my A-levels, was 'Das Kapital' (Volume 1) by Karl Marx.

I made friends with several white friends who were from a more diverse working class mix than at Aston. At least three have stayed close friends over the five decades since then and a few others I still get cards from and have met up over the years. To some extent as Asian students, we were also living a dual existence with our white friends, switching codes, and behaving in ways that suited the occasion and context. I was always really into disco, soul, and Motown music primarily as it allowed me to dance the nights away at the Student Union. In my first year at Kingston, I was again in a girls' university residence in Surbiton where I became friends with Jane. We were an unlikely pair in that she was shy, but neither of us were into alcohol although we enjoyed the social side. Kathy, a Welsh Sociology student, and I used to dance a lot. It was the happiest time dancing until closing time.

To an extent we all were adjusting and switching personas no matter what we were studying. We were juggling multiple identities. Many young people from South Asian families still straddle these identities in modern Britain in 2020's but the context for some is even more complex than for my generation. I listen to young people discussing sexuality and LGBTQ+ issues. My 'liberal' generation, often the parents now to a new generation, bring their own prejudices, religion or politics, which can still be controlling and therefore warrant use of multiple identities for our offspring. We, the parents, are possibly repressive in other ways in the context of our children's lives. Of course, this is not the preserve of South Asian families as we know.

However, the gendered perspectives I had encountered in my family began to change over time. In other words, the way girls' and women's roles were being interpreted began to change, albeit slowly. This is not to say that wider society changed from a patriarchal to a more egalitarian one, but in my own family real change came when my brothers had daughters of their own, a little later. Having daughters consciously or unconsciously changed their attitudes and aspirations for that generation, which hopefully would not limit their life chances. This was particularly so in education and in more latitude in choosing life partners.

For example, all my nieces were encouraged and enabled to study. They had support and opportunities to use education to progress rather than being hindered by the threat of marriage throughout their early lives. In my Leicester family I was the first to set aspirations for myself, and among my peers there were only about three of us Gujarati girls from my neighbourhood who left home and found a place to grow and flourish through higher and further education. Today, to some extent the wider changes in society have also created a better climate for changing attitudes. For my generation, the treatment of East African Asian girls by their families, expecting them to succeed and be ambitious had a positive effect for some of us. In turn, this helped the subsequent generation of Indian girls including my own daughters and nieces. I was liberated by observing the difference in attitude of the opportunities for those girls afforded by their families, notably Renu's family at A-levels. I saw this was available to me (if I was careful) and that was a strong motivation to later apply for a university place.

On return from India, Mum went back to work in a hosiery mill. Suresh had completed his course in London and started working full-time for a firm in Leicester. Mum then focussed on helping find a bride for him and a groom for me. Within our community it was still very daunting and patriarchal for a young widow to be undertaking this on her own. Trying to initially get two of her three children married at this stage was going to be difficult without a male partner to support the process. Meanwhile, I came home in July 1977 after graduating, ready to see what the future had in store for me. I was going to 'face the music' of matrimony and was ready to see if I could make things work. Having a social science degree should have given my family and others a clue that I did not really want a traditional conventional marriage – arranged or otherwise. Meeting women who were critical of the traditional women's role, questioning the institution of marriage, along with the influence of the women's movement helped me to be clearer of where I should be heading.

I remember undergoing one 'interview' with a potential suitor during my postgraduate period at home. After serving him and his family with chai, dressed in my sari (usually how young women were expected to behave) he asked me what my ambitions were for myself, rather than could I cook! He could see I was not interested in a conventional marriage and urged me to stick to my ambition for a life I wanted. We had an interesting chat and wished each other well. He was one of the more enlightened ones. I saw others over the years from the age of seventeen to about twenty-five to comply with expectations, but each one left me in despair. I had lived that parallel life I spoke of earlier.

I had relationships with white men whilst at Kingston and later during my postgraduate course. I did not meet Indian men who I felt romantically drawn to, or indeed them to me. Like all relationships, mine were exciting, dull, or painful – especially in late teens and early twenties when everyone is trying to find themselves. It was a useful time for me to grow as a person since at home I had been made to feel unattractive. This was because in those days my brothers and even my Mum had a stereotype of what a desirable woman should look like for marriage prospects (a Bollywood actor possibly), rather than seeing the whole person. It was a sexist interpretation, and I suffered especially during my adolescence and before leaving home. Going to university I discovered I was fun, interesting, bright and even attractive.

Leaving home was the making of me. I cannot imagine I would have grown as an individual without the freedom I got the moment I finished my A-levels and the subsequent opportunities I created for myself. Because marriage per se was not an end goal, I was not interested in running away with anyone. Unfortunately, families of young girls in my community were preoccupied with a notion that we all wanted to run away with a man! Ideally, I wanted to pursue my interests. Liberated from the strict codes of behaviour and thought, I discovered that I had quite a contemporary and progressive interpretation of life that inspired me and helped me look forward to life, rather than stopping the clock at eighteen when I felt I would be shackled by marriage and domestic work.

Generally, my feminism and politics were now more consolidated by my studies, especially in sociology. It really helped me not to confuse romantic love with marriage as an institution. It is true that the brand of feminism that influenced me was not good at taking on race or class perspectives, but I was aware and critical of that aspect. However, I was at that time also clear that I would not do anything to upset the family. I never wanted to hurt Mum in any way. I knew, in the end, she wanted the best for me but based on her own experience and knowledge. This was limited to the rather narrow world view of male and female roles in a Prajapati community for much of my childhood.

I also knew and felt that my Mum was becoming much more liberal as Dad was not alive to assert his extraordinarily strong views, and by this time she was immensely proud that I was a graduate and was proud of my tenacity and resilience. She had come to my graduation ceremony, and it moved her that, despite the odds, I had made it happen. She had sat in the audience with Suresh and my friend Annie's mum, who had held my Mum's hand as a gesture of shared pride as two working class women. Annie is still a great friend; she came from an Irish working-class family, from a London council estate and went on to do a PhD and become an academic in the field of teacher education and training.

Mum has often shared her regret at not supporting me more when I was younger and wondered what paths or other choices I may have taken if I had been offered a wider berth. I began to understand early on that you could ask the same questions of my Mum's life. What would she have done if she was not hampered by English language and had access to opportunities like those I had? This reframing helped me understand my Mum's life and the world from her perspective once I left home and was not just preoccupied by my life course.

Graduation and leaving home

The degree was indeed the bargaining chip I had hoped it would be, and Mum began to think the suitors were not good enough for me because I had more to bring to a potential marriage. Mum was now more understanding of the role parents had in enabling girls to aim higher for all things in life. By now, I also wanted to experience the world and seek a career and fulfilment in other ways and not just through marriage and relationships. I wanted things that were very normal for someone who was looking to build an independent life. However, these few months after graduation in Leicester was to give my Mum an opportunity to make one last attempt at a suitable match, and for me to be seen to be fair to her for supporting me to go away for three years. But it did not happen.

After the graduation ceremony at Kingston Polytechnic 1977, now Kingston University

Eventually after a few months of unemployment in Leicester, I applied for a job in Manchester to do residential work in a probation hostel. It was a new initiative to have residential bail and probation hostels run by the Probation Service. It would give me good practical experience required for the social work course which I had decided I would pursue as a career and provide accommodation at the same time. Work focussed on criminal justice interested me most, so this did tick many boxes. Even Mum was relieved I was going as I had been so unhappy back in Leicester living at home. Just before I left, Suresh took me for a meal to ask me what I wanted to do with my future. As an older brother he was standing in for my dad. He also wanted clarification so he could go ahead and plan his own marriage. I suggested he did what was right for him, and I went away still not sure how my life was going to pan out but excited to be leaving home again to at least plan for a career and with a structure for the immediate future. The spectre of arranged marriage still cast a shadow over me for a few more years to come and I accepted that it might still happen – but increasingly if it did, I felt it would be more on my terms.

The probation hostel work was demanding residential work with a lot of challenges, but I made good friends with the other residential staff – the Warden, senior probation officer and his family, and the Deputy Warden and his family. They became an extended family for me. I was an Assistant Warden alongside Lois who did not 'live in' as she had a house in Manchester but would sleep in for her overnight duties. She became a good friend too and along with her house-mate Hazel and her partner Doug. Manchester was a lively and an exciting place, and Lois introduced me to its more glamorous side, with new music, networks, and a whole new approach to find clothes from charity shops. She was arty and a refreshing person. I loved Manchester but after 20 months I applied for professional social work course at Southampton University – it was for one year, so I was saving a year of training since the course at Manchester University was for two years.

My brothers' marriages

Suresh and Mum eventually found a marriage partner for him whilst I was in Manchester, and in May 1978 he got married. Chandra and I came home for the wedding. My Bhabhi-to-be (Sumitra), a young Indian bride from Walsall in the Midlands, was still in her teens. Both Mum and Suresh were stressed by the process as they had to undertake all the arrangements themselves without a father-figure or husband to help. There are politics and diplomacy involved in finding suitable partners and often there is an intermediary who introduces prospective partners to the interested family. There was always some pressure to take the process forward smoothly. Parents wanted firm commitment on both sides and an agreement; they worried that if a 'contract' was not forthcoming soon, then it could get difficult and risky. There would be serious reputational damage if the agreement was broken, or arrangements stalled for any reason. There is an amusing story line in 'Bend it Like Beckham' (film directed by Gurinder Charda, 2002) which illustrates this point. Here, Jess' sister's wedding is nearly cancelled because her prospective in-laws mistakenly think Jess is kissing a white boy in the street, which reflects badly on the family. It nearly leads to the cancellation of her sister's wedding. Although depicted as a comedy, in real life this would have serious consequences. Our wider Prajapati family were still very traditional and as a widow my Mum was feeling under pressure to get my brother settled, now that he had completed his studies and was working.

Suresh's wedding party (jan) went from Leicester to Walsall (the place of the bride's home) to a community hall. It followed a pattern adopted by many. We took a coachful of people to the wedding, all catered and provided for by the bride's side. Mum was able to present the things she had brought from India – saris, gold jewellery, woollen shawls, and money. Relatives and friends contributed money as wedding presents and both sides recorded the money in a register. Nowadays they all make it clear that 'no boxed gifts please'. The recording of money given as a wedding present is an important consideration for wedding party guests to 'repay' similar amounts when the time comes for a reciprocal opportunity.

I remember the bethak the next day. Usually, the bethak is for close extended family only, and although Hindus can be strict vegetarians, we are a meat-eating family so we would eat meat post-sacred wedding period. The men had bottles of beer and spirits, and some of the older women may have had a little beer, but it was soft drinks of Coca Cola for most of us women. Usually, the period leading to the wedding would be meat-free including the actual wedding day as it was considered a sacred period. I have always loved bethak at any close family weddings because it is a little like post-Christmas Day when all the pressure is off. We could relax and relatives could share jokes and enjoy being with each other (if there had not been major fallouts or incidents). It was time to calm any of the tensions that may have been exposed. Since bethak is a family occasion, I enjoyed the warmth and glow of a communal gathering with relatives from near and far. The bhajias always smelled and tasted even better than usual, and the goat sak was always aromatic and tastier on these occasions. Somehow all the love, care and sharing in those days, mingled with scents of incense and chrysanthemum flowers together with the power struggles of family members for roles of importance in the ceremony was a dynamic mix to the actual wedding. The women relatives who helped cook in tiny kitchens or hired gas burners and large pots of different sak were skilled in cooking for large volumes of people. They did a wonderful job but there was an element of competition as to who made the tastiest food! A bit of rivalry and teasing was allowed amongst the older women relatives at weddings including singing rude songs about the in-laws on both the groom's and the bride's side. It could get racy at times, and a departure from the normal decorum and respect to which we were all taught to adhere.

I remember our garden wall in Leicester had fallen, and the bricks were in a pile in the tiny yard. But people spilled over and just sat outside on these bricks and made merry. Our neighbours, the Overheads, were (luckily for us) very tolerant people and did not complain. I cannot quite imagine that scenario now with my family. The ability to just make the most of what was on offer and go with the flow was quite acceptable back then. The weddings now are very formal affairs with restrictive guest lists, and mostly ceremonies are held in elaborate venues outside the home with caterers, many changes of outfits for the bride and adaptations to suit every pocket and circumstances. Incredible amounts of money are spent – in many ways not hugely different to the general trend in all communities in Britain. Adaptation now includes stag nights and elaborate hen-parties in our Indian and Prajapati circles. Unfortunately for me and Chandra, there are now restrictive practices of invitation, and we do not get invited to 'family' weddings. In our family, only Suresh as the oldest in our sibling group gets invited to the wedding (with Bhabhi – my sister-in-law) as the representative of the family. Mum still gets invited, but she is not able to go so Suresh usually takes his younger daughter in her place.

We were still living in our house in Wingfield Street with an outside toilet and shower room in the coal shed in the yard until 1981. The family moved to Braunstone when my niece was born, and they needed a bigger house with at least an inside bathroom. They bought a three bedroomed semi with a large garden and a garage. Moving out of the Melton Road/Belgrave area was always a goal for families who migrated to that area in the 1960s. It was a mixture of wanting a larger house with more amenities and a desire to show upward mobility. White people had steadily moved out as our Asian population started to move into the area. Braunstone did not have the greatest reputation as it was on a large council estate (one of the largest in the country I believe) but the new house was on the edge of the estate in a residential street with semi-detached housing and large gardens. Mum gave up her home that my dad had bought, and we had grown up in. It was a dark dispiriting house but had seen us through. My Mum split the proceedings amongst us and relinquished her own property and financial security to live with the eldest son. She saw her role as servicing the family and supporting her older son's family as tradition expected. The roles designated for the mother and daughter-in-law were unwritten but totally accepted at the time. This was the prescribed role of a widow with sons, and not unusual - it was a natural progression for her to live with her eldest son and his wife. Chandra and I saw the new house as an extension of Wingfield Street as Mum was still our central figure. Suresh, as the married eldest son, was by implication head of the family.

Just after Suresh's wedding, Chandra was establishing his medical career. Chandra was waiting to impart his news about his relationship but was waiting until I had 'settled' into an arranged marriage. He did not want to jeopardise my chances as his decision and choices could have an impact on any potential arranged marriage for me. However, it was clear that I was not going to do any 'settling' in the immediate future. Things came to a head when Chandra, who had been seen as the most traditional out of us three (through expression of his views and values at the time) told us he would be marrying a white woman who had a 4-year-old son.

Chandra and Pat married soon after he graduated which caused a great commotion for my immediate and the extended family. Qualifying as a doctor brought significant social status for any Indian family in the 1970s. As we came from a rural Gujarati family, it was a triumph that Chandra had reached this pinnacle, securing a role as a medical doctor by qualifying at an English University. It was a real achievement in those days when taken in context of racism, classism, and the lack of support from the educational establishment. Chandra graduated from St Mary's Medical School in London in 1976.

The Prajapatis had been enormously proud of Chandra and were invested in him as an example of what we could achieve in England. Within our immediate extended family, there was disappointment that the first qualified doctor in our 'family' would marry 'outside the Jati' (community) – especially to a non-Indian and non-Hindu white woman with a child. This was a massive deal for Mum who was still a woman framed by the values of our community and its expectations. At that time, a son becoming a doctor should have given her pride and status but instead she became a target of pity and derision. His plans to marry sent shockwaves in our immediate Prajapati family in India too. There was a feeling of betrayal. Clearly Chandra was leading a dual existence like the rest of us; the transition we were undergoing with education, opportunities, life choices and experiences were affecting all of us including Mum. She had no control over this scenario. Although Mum was daunted and troubled, her understanding and resilience was particularly important now and prevented those around us from dividing our family unit.

Although Mum proved to be strong and stoical, we know it was a very difficult time for her and there was an element of losing some honour amongst the wider community as we were the first 'villagers' to step out of the norms and values of marriage and kinship. My extended family did not help as they were very much rooted in the traditions, and they showed their disquiet without providing support. A few turned up for Chandra's wedding at the registry office but without much joy. As my new sister-in-law, Pat, was a practising Catholic, they had a church blessing, then Sumitrabhabhi, helped dress her in a royal blue silk sari (given by Mum) for the couple to get blessings at the temple too. We, as the immediate family members, united in supporting Chandra and Pat and little James. In a way it was a 'very modern marriage' in the context of a difficult atmosphere.

Once Chandra had married unconventionally (and later Peter and I did so too) there was an element of Suresh and Sumitra holding the Prajapati mantle and feeling they had conformed and were living within the community norms. To a degree, I felt they held the moral high ground for a decade or so until Mum had to leave what was her shared home with her son and family.

Of course, times have changed so much that marrying out of caste and jati, and marrying a white person is not now a major issue in most urban and educated, middle class households in the Prajapati community. In fact, it can be a cause for celebration, having fusion ceremonies with different approaches to the wedding, food and rituals. People enjoy bringing the different strands of wedding cultures and religious elements together. I have seen both parties with their parents at sari shops buying things for different ceremonies on Belgrave Road. But this was the late 1970's and early 80's, and people would have discussed and enjoyed gossiping about our family. Many households probably had a very detailed discussions about our family at the time, with Mum being seen as the 'poor widow' who had to endure this humiliation.

Our generation, particularly the ones accessing higher education, were increasingly exposed to wider influences and experiences. However, most young Indian students were still encouraged to study science, engineering, pharmacy and dentistry or business and economics, were still relatively conservative influences. Many of our peers at the time (even some accessing higher education) were still marrying within our jati, so our family was considered unusual once the news of Chandra's relationship was known.

Thankfully, despite the hurt she must have felt from the extended family, Mum did have the good sense to support Chandra and not banish him (or, later, me). That is what some parents resorted to, casting their son or daughter out totally from the family and their networks. In all honesty, had my Dad been alive, things may have turned out very differently for all of us. It is highly likely we would not have opposed him. If we had, we would have been cut adrift. Mum certainly would not have gone against his views. Ironically, being a widow gave her more scope to be understanding of her children and support them. As well as our community being a very patriarchal society, Dad was from a very traditional mould of very controlling men. He did mellow through his illness, but had he not had a stroke, it is hard to envisage him changing enough to embrace our very different lives. What would we have done had our Dad been alive when we made those major life decisions? It is too difficult to contemplate, and it is important to acknowledge how much leeway Mum gave us in the end. Was it because she found it difficult to hold out against our life choices or was she adapting to the changing world around her in a more considered way? Her ability to understand us and change her attitude over these crucial years kept us together as a family. I know her attitude to me and to my aspirations changed over time and changed our relationship greatly for the better.

As for marrying into the Muslim faith, neither community would tolerate it. At the time there were a couple of young women in Leicester who married Muslim men, and they were totally ostracised. That religious combination is still very much an issue and worthy of a separate discussion, but worth noting, as well as the thorny issue of marriage between Indian and Black partners of African or Caribbean heritage. This is noticeably changing in our Prajapati communities, reflecting a natural evolution to a more globally diverse Britain. In 1993 Gurinder Charda directed a film 'Bhaji on the Beach', written by Meera Syal, which addressed those earlier prejudices and experiences across our cultures; I believe this combination of 'mixed marriages' is becoming more acceptable in a similar way our family's marriages were initially seen as problematic by some Prajapati's but has now become normalised.

The other important topic is the significant change in British society in relation to gender, sexuality and those considered 'alternative' lifestyles and how this is seen and dealt with by different generations of Desis. It is hard to appreciate the scale of acceptability by the wider Asian diaspora on issues of LGBTQ+. We know that in all our societies there are varying degrees of acknowledgment and openness. Much of this is also determined by religion and a certain level of liberalism through education, further studies and expanding career choices including the arts, theatre, and fashion within our Asian communities. The career choices and interests are more diverse - no longer the narrow field considered acceptable as before. Furthermore, the influence of new technology and social media has had a critical impact on all our societies.

In the last 25 years, even before the rise of social media and 'Millenials', our offspring were diversifying from the traditional professions to which their parents aspired. There are an increasing range of professions and opportunities in the 'creative' industries, which none of us would have considered or been allowed to enter. These might not have been accessible because of race, misogyny, or class barriers. Such choices have a profound impact on how individuals interpret and change the world, and they allow young people to challenge ideologies and traditions, including culture. Amongst the offspring of my immediate family there is significant diversification, including a wildlife film producer, a dancer turned housing expert engaged in addressing homelessness, a successful actor turned smallholding farmer, an artist, and others working in marketing, graphics, web design and as influencers. At the same time, there is continuity in the medical profession with a hard-working consultant doctor, now supporting our NHS that is even more fragile than the one experienced before by Chandra.

Prajapatis have never been a homogeneous group – and have become less so as we have settled into a more complex society, with global migration creating even greater diversity in the population. We are still very much in our infancy in supporting people who do not fit in with heterosexual or straight relationships in a range of our communities despite new laws on civil partnerships and marriages in Britain. I am sure many younger Asians are living with dual and multiple identities and leading parallel lives even more complicated than some of us did some years ago.

Becoming a professional probation officer

I never went back to Leicester to live after leaving Manchester. I moved to Southampton University to do a post-graduate social work qualification. I got a Home Office sponsorship so then went to work in the Probation Service; this was a positive choice for me and my work in the probation hostel had given me an excellent grounding. In the 1980's, the Probation Service was working with offenders to provide an alternative to prison and supporting offenders both in prison and after their release, using criminal justice and social work approaches and frameworks. I considered it to be an exciting organisation to work for. Our Union – The National Association of Probation Officers (NAPO) – promoted a progressive element in our profession and professional practice. I became a member of the National Training Committee on NAPO some years later. The General Secretary of NAPO, Bill Beaumont, later came to Bristol University as a lecturer, where we became colleagues and taught and researched on the probation side of the professional Social Work Course.

The Probation Service was rooted in the work of the old court missionaries. The service was based around a region and had locality-based offices serving the local population. The focus of the work when I trained was on rehabilitation of offenders and helping to address the wider determinants leading to offending behaviour. The emphasis was on supporting the individual to find employment, housing, education and training, offering counselling and therapeutic approaches as well as practical groups. Individuals were linked with networks and resources, including those that helped manage drugs and alcohol misuse. Unfortunately, political interference, cuts and privatisation have totally undermined the service and the profession; many of us no longer recognise the service. It became a national organisation and had huge problems with an ever-increasing workload, so the work of probation officers has become ever more pressurised. Most importantly, the training infrastructure for qualification was dismantled and taken out of higher education sector. Officers are trained using competence, risk-based models, stripping out the academic underpinning of the social sciences – a key aspect of the professional course alongside skills-based two-year training. Public outcry, pressure on the service, increasing risks and overcrowding in prisons has led to reorganisation again and we watch with interest and see how it evolves.

After Southampton, I had a difficult two-year post-qualification period in Redditch where I struggled to settle. The team was part of Hereford and Worcester Probation Service so encompassed both a rural and more urban catchment. I had chosen Redditch as opposed to Worcester as I wanted to work with young people. One positive thing about Redditch (a new town on the edge of Birmingham) was that my friendship with a student from Southampton, Janet, became established. Neither of us were happy with our circumstances, she with her job and me with my location. I resolved to move to a city and focus on my career and she too amended her future work plans but liked Birmingham so bought her first house in Kings Heath. We also planned to go on a big journey to India, no matter what our circumstances. We pledged to do this within two years and gave each other the undertaking that we would adhere to the timescale. I wanted to explore my heritage and was increasingly interested in racism and anti-racism in the British context. I was keen to reconnect with India and understand British colonialism through my heritage and as a British Asian. Janet was keen to have her own experience and adventures in India with a friend who had migrated from there.

By this time, Mum and my brothers were clearer that I would not be happy in any kind of an arranged marriage. My Mum realised that it would cause her more problems than it would solve! I was in a relationship with a white man, and did not actively hide this; certainly, Suresh and Mum were aware of it. The relationship was in its last stages as in June 1982 I moved to Bristol, so it was not significant for my future.

Within six months of moving to Bristol in June 1982 and settling in my job with Avon Probation Service, I bought my first house. So in January 1983 - almost 20 years to the day from arriving in England as a 7-year-old, I got the keys to my Victorian house. I sat alone in my large empty lounge and promised myself that I would draw a line in the sand. Buying a house on my own was a symbol of my independence and a fresh start.

Joining the Labour Party: politics and activism

By 1982 I had become involved in the Labour Party. I had a chance to attend a conference in West Berlin organised by the British Council on a German British exchange programme. I had been recommended by a colleague in Redditch to the British Council as a participant. On arriving at Avon Probation, I took annual leave to attend as it was considered prestigious, attracting people considered as potential candidates for future leadership. I met exciting young professionals working in media and journalism, political parties and business, and we were allowed to go into East Berlin through Checkpoint Charlie to attend the 'Threepenny Opera' at the Berliner Ensemble. The wall dividing East and West Berlin was very much the reason that NATO (North Atlantic Treaty Organisation) supported this conference. I assume there was an underlying message but whatever it was, I found it most inspiring for the people I met.

The focus of discussion was the future of the media and the role of innovative technology. I was a bit out of my depth, but it was all very stimulating and pertinent to the world we live in now. I met people from all parts of the political spectrum including from the newly formed SDP (Social Democratic Party) and journalists from broadsheets such as the Financial Times. There were also radical Labour councillors from Sheffield who were part of the movement for municipal socialism in the early 1980's. Their passion and commitment were infectious and built on my desire to get more politically involved and to work for equality and justice. As a result, on my return home I joined the Labour Party in my constituency of East Bristol. A colleague at my Probation Office was Janet Cocks (by then divorced from Michael Cocks, Labour MP for Bristol South) who took me to my first meeting. My MP was the veteran left-wing Tony Benn. I had a friend who was a colleague lodging with me, and together we canvassed for Tony Benn at the 1983 election, but our constituency boundary had been redrawn and as a result he lost his seat after serving as an MP for Bristol South East since 1950.

My friend Clare and I drowned our sorrows with gin and tonic as the news came in, but we were new to the whole issue of party politics at that time, so took it in our stride. Later, once I was more involved, I would find the defeats at elections very painful and upsetting. Clare went on to work for a large homelessness charity in London and years later after working in related fields, was made a Dame. She came from a very upper-class family who were socially and politically well-connected. However, we had a similar political outlook, and she encouraged me to go out with Peter who was our Branch Secretary and the District Secretary of the Labour Party. I was really enjoying my time in Bristol with my new job and colleagues in Easton area of Bristol and a growing friendship circle. Political activism came naturally to me – years of fighting against injustice just made harnessing that energy into social and political action very productive and gave me an edge in my professional work too.

There had been unrest in the St Paul's and Easton areas of Bristol, with rebellions by young Black people during early 1980's – mainly against the policing and surveillance of the Black communities. As a result, there was a great deal of community work taking place with officers from the two Probation Offices leading on community partnerships with a range of agencies including the police. By 1984 I was much more absorbed in the Labour Party and sympathetic to industrial struggles going on at the time, especially the mining communities, which the Thatcher Government had set out to destroy. During the ensuing miner's strike, I was interested in the role of the women, both from within the mining community and from outside, and how working-class women were taking leadership activity and roles within wider movements. I was also, through the Labour Movement, becoming an activist on several fronts – from women's rights and reproductive rights, the Anti-Apartheid movement and the boycott of South African goods and services. Struggles in support of Nelson Mandela's freedom from imprisonment in South Africa was something many of my generation were engaged in for many years until his release in February 1990. At the Labour Women's conferences in the mid 80's we met very inspiring Black African and South African women activists who came to speak. Supporting the women at Greenham Common peace camps by taking food and provisions was a minor contribution on my part but for those of us that did not or could not camp, it allowed us to show solidarity.

Back to India, 21 years on

With all this, a new relationship and emerging new friendships, Janet and I kept to our plans for travelling and went to India at the end of September 1984. We were committed to going; three months for me and a little longer than that for Janet as she planned to do a work-related placement at the end. I took paid and unpaid leave and Janet cashed in her superannuation to fund her trip. Mum had gone on her second visit and was there waiting for us – it was good to have her there as a bridge to my relatives and to Gujarat itself. Suresh, Peter, my friends from Kingston and a couple of colleagues came to see me off at Heathrow and were incredibly supportive, recognising I was going back for the first time since we migrated. It seemed a big deal to all of us at the time.

I was keen to go back to India before I was thirty as I knew my family would all be concerned that I was not married. It was twenty-one years since our migration to England, and I was excited to go back with my friend who knew me in a wholly different context as a professional woman in England.

On our arrival at the airport in what was Bombay (Mumbai) in 1984 there was hustle and bustle, and we were shocked by people living in shacks just off the runway. Meeting my Ajima, my Manekmama and Mum at the airport was so emotional. The journey from the airport to Navsari was full of incidents and surprises, with a blown tyre and stops for food and drinks on the way. Reconnecting with my home village Munsad, the Navsari district and my relatives as well as travelling around Desh was special. Having Janet with me to share my experiences was great. She understood how emotional the whole experience was for me and my relatives and was a wonderful observer, recorder and confidant during those three months.

We were an oddity for my relatives, not just as an Indian and an English friend who were both British – but they saw independent, young professional women who were interested in the minutiae of the Gujarati life. They were amused by us at the beginning but found us more interesting as they got to understand our motives. They were not familiar with the backpacking fraternity and certainly not a Gujarati and white woman being slightly off-beat in 1984. We looked an unlikely pair as Janet was a lot taller than my five foot, so we were a bit like 'little and large.' Around Navsari people stared at us as we went for our walks. At that time Navsari did not have any white visitors as it was not part of any tourist trail.

Ajima and Mum arranged for us to have space in the top flat of the new building my uncle had built for the family. My family had lived in extremely poor conditions when we lived there before but their fortunes had changed. Navsari was the centre of the developing diamond-cutting industry. I am not sure I approved of the ethics of the diamond trade then or now but that is what was helping the boom in the city. Ajima had paid for my Manekmama to be apprenticed and train. He took to it well and quickly acquired a reputation for his skill.

Janet on the roof of the building of Aradhana – the house built to accommodate all the Mamas' (Mum's brothers and their families)

When we woke up in the morning Mum and Ajima would do their chores and make us food and talk. These chats could go either way; they could be happy and joking or become tearful and sad depending on the topic. As we talked in Gujarati, Janet could not predict which way these chats would go but was incredibly sensitive to letting us just get on – using her power of observation and appropriate body language to show she was in tune with what was going on for us. The social work training really helped here. Occasionally she would snap a photo capturing the moment. This was in the days before camera phones, but she had a small Cannon SLR that she carried around. We would then go down a floor where my Rukhimami lived with her family. My Maganmama (uncle) had died of kidney failure and left his young wife with four children. She would feed us our second breakfast and make a fuss of us. She is the funniest and rudest of all my aunts and we loved that about her. And there would be more chats. There were two more families on the way down; with Kishormama and Gitamami and their three children, and then Manekmama and Pushpamami and their three children who all fed us and helped us to plan our day. Janet and I were the first set of visitors from England who did not lose weight! We were very polite and did not want to offend them and ate even when we were full. We have so many photos which seem to say: 'Can I really eat another mouthful?' We realised that when my relatives came to visit us in England, they didn't seem bound by same desire to please us and would often refuse any extra treats we tried to encourage them to take. We were such pushovers compared to them.

Ajima preparing flowers for her prayers

Mum and Ajima doing chores in the morning

Visiting Munsad was very emotional as I remembered our house, the village, the neighbourhood, and school.

Man with hay on head and the scene which greeted us in Munsad in 1984

Both my Laduma and Bhulima (who we had lived with) had died in the intervening years. As youngsters we were all so excited by leaving India to go to England, we had not considered that we may not see some of our relatives again. Our share of the family home had been sold to my cousin, and it was being rented by a family. There were photos on the wall of Suresh and Sumitra's wedding that we had sent, and old pictures of my Makanbapa with his bhajan (singing) group from South Africa, which I refer to in Part 1. I took away this faded photo as I knew it would just disappear if I did not rescue it. My widowed aunt, Diwalima, was alive and still living with her sons in Munsad. It was good to see that side of our family life – those who stayed and could not migrate doing well economically and socially enjoying life. We were all indoctrinated to think that migrating was the only way out of poverty or extremely low income. I did meet an old school friend, and it made me wonder how my life would have been different if we had never left India - or if my Dad had sent me back with Mum to look after my Laduma and Bhulima as he was planning when he had a stroke.

At Diwalima's house we were invited to lunch and her daughter in law, Chanchanbhabhi was making puris for us

Being able to communicate in Gujarati really helped me to bond with people and I was pleasantly surprised how they felt I had turned out. They were indeed worried I was not yet married, but proud of my educational achievements and independence. In terms of education, the people in Munsad were proud of the early years we had had at the village as they felt the foundations of my learning had been established in India. We saw my tiny old village school, that was now closed.

The old school was in a dilapidated state after 21 years

The authorities had built a new school, and we went along to see the pupils and teachers. The school was huge, by the old standards, and seemed to be thriving.

Having my own income and house and treating them to gifts, money and beers (acquired with our 'liquor permits') symbolised my independence and my difference as an Indian woman, to the one they had expected. It made me realise how important the early years spent in India were in shaping my relationships with my aunts, uncles, and relatives and India itself. I had a history there and it felt critical for me to reconnect the bonds

I thought may have broken. Being able to speak Gujarati seemed to be the most important aspect of this bonding process. But it was also a revelation to me in the way migration had led to so much loss – leaving a homeland, our language, our relatives, identity and the sense of the right to belong. I also realised that in the process of our loss, we had also created a loss for relatives we had 'abandoned.' This would be a recurring theme for me and my Mum for years to come.

In time, cousins from both Mum and Dad's side of the family would join us in England or go on to the USA or Canada via their education, skills or via marriage arrangements. Many of them were older adults before moving abroad but they all adapted and settled. At the time, the lure of 'the West' was so powerful and in some ways, it still is despite India's place in the world as a leading economic powerhouse. My impression is that unless you are from a wealthy family the desire to move to 'the West' is still strong within my relatives and Prajapatis because it presents opportunities that India does not afford to lower income people with little inherited wealth. Even when wealth or middle-class status is acquired in India, the desire to buy your way into the West through a legitimate route to England or Canada is often the preferred option.

Janet and I took my Mum to Mount Abu, Udaipur, and Jaipur on our own, and using the Lonely Planet guide we stayed in accommodation that was sometimes nice, but sometimes dubious.

Mum and I waiting at a bus station during our trip to Mount Abu

Strolling along the beach at Daman

To compensate for the shoddy place in Udaipur, we took her for afternoon tea at Lake Palace Hotel. We spent hours there and Mum talked to Janet about her life as I translated, and we enjoyed a little bit of extravagance which Mum would not normally experience. It also helped her understand that when we went off travelling on our own around India, she could feel that we were sensible and safe. We returned to Navsari and visited more relatives before embarking again on our travels, backpacking from Bombay where our family waved us goodbye, a little bemused by the notion of us travelling around with rucksacks.

Armed with only our Lonely Planet Guide to India we set off. This was in the days of no mobile phones, no bottled water, and no online booking of comfortable trains. We had to change our route plan – our carefully worked out schedule to travel north and then south was abandoned as Indira Ghandhi, then Prime Minister, was assassinated just as our travels commenced at Bombay. Riots broke out in Delhi, and it was unsafe, so we changed course entirely. As India went into meltdown we were stopped by the police and searched but luckily allowed to carry on our travels. It was a great upheaval, and a little bit scary to change our planned route to avoid the chaos. We decided to reverse the direction of travel and explore South India first and then go to the North, hoping the violence and turbulence of recent weeks would subside. Our family and friends in England and India were not sure where we were and were really worried about our welfare following the news bulletins. Using phones was a nightmare in 1984, even within India, often not being able to connect because of some spurious reason, equivalent to 'leaves on the line'

It turned out to be a great adventure, and we experienced the highs and lows of travelling around with limited resources but also splashing out on an odd hotel or two, eating at a nicer restaurant when the going got tough. I struggled with the 'bathroom situation' on our long journeys on buses as initially we just could not get on the trains. Janet was much better than me coping with that aspect. It was clear that I was often seen by Indians as 'Indian' because of the colour of my skin and black hair but was treated as a 'foreigner' too. This was because of my dress, attitude, lack of Hindi and I spoke English with an English accent. Janet was often treated with some deference depending on which part of India we were travelling through.

We met some interesting people, both from England and other parts of the world, travelling and doing the similar routes to ours in the south and the 'Golden Triangle' of the north. They were mainly white tourists doing the journeys for a variety of reasons: from desire to experience something new, to spiritual enlightenment, to just travelling before settling down. Some were kindred spirits, but some people were totally ignorant of the impact of British colonialism/imperialism and the relationship with the right to British citizenship for those who migrated to England. We did meet people who were using racist tropes about Asians in Britain and wondered why they were in India at all. Generally, we were the only combination of white and Asian women travelling and caused many to stare at us. But it was good that Janet and I were able to discuss all this on our long journeys. I met a young Indian woman who was a medical student on one of these long train rides. She was fascinated by our trip and asked what I would do eventually. I guess she felt that if I did still marry according to the cultural expectations, I would be no better off than her or any other educated Indian woman. Basically, servicing the family was something I was putting off, she said. These interludes gave me pause for thought but I did not tell her that I was probably not going down the arranged marriage route now. It was good to have those talks as it helped me get a perspective on things.

Janet and I discussed both the Labour Party and the Tory Government under Margaret Thatcher. Peter was writing long letters about what was going on back home politically, but I did not get these letters on my travels. On my return to Navsari, I found my Ajima had collected them and locked them up in her suitcase as she did not trust my aunts and uncles not to have a peek. Peter sent very bulky letters in envelopes, but my relatives would have been extremely disappointed as Peter was sending me notice of Labour Party meetings with the agenda and minutes – taking his responsibility as a Labour Party Branch Secretary seriously! The relatives had cottoned-on that I had a special friend and my mamis were all anxious to find out more on my return.

We enjoyed the south, visiting Goa, Kerala including the Periyar National Park, Tamil Nadu, Bangalore and Madras (Chennai). We were disappointed when we got to the southern tip at Kanya Kumari where we were expecting to experience the miracle of sunset and sunrise; it was overcast and did not live up to our expectations. We made our way to the north on an overnight train journey via Hyderabad to Delhi. We went through Bhopal, little knowing that it was the place where the Union Carbide disaster was to unfold soon after on the night of 2-3 December 1984. We saw the erotic temples of Khajuraho, the beautiful Rajasthan landscape and people and visited the 'Golden Triangle'. We really were mesmerised by the Taj Mahal at Agra and felt the spiritual pull of Varanasi where for a moment I got very emotional about my Dad and his ashes having been scattered in the sacred Ganges. As we travelled to the foothills of the Himalayas towards Rishikesh we found the bridge,

Laxman Jhula, a bit disappointing. I had expected it to be much more impressive but monkeys at either end of the bridge really frightened me.

Tara and Janet at Laxman Jhula/ Ganges

If Indira Gandhi had not been assassinated our original plan had been to go through Chandigarh, Amritsar, through Punjab and then to Shimla, the hill station to which the British used to retreat from the summer heat. But the route had been closed due to the assassination and to this day I have not managed to get to Punjab or to Shimla. We went to Ahmedabad and visited Gandhi's place of residence on the Sabarmati River and a museum in which the timeline of events for the struggle for Independence was laid out. Janet and I talked a lot about British Imperialism, the displacement and death of citizens with the awful events leading to the partitioning of India and Pakistan and eventual Independence.

At the end of six weeks of travelling non-stop, Janet and I celebrated my 29th birthday in a 'Quality Hotel' in Dehra Dunn. We decided we had come to the end of our travels and headed back home on a very long journey via Delhi to Surat and then a bus to Navsari. Our family were surprised to see us, bedraggled, hair full of dust, and looking weary arriving on their doorstep. They had expected to pick us up in Surat or Ahmedabad, but we decided just to make our own way. They were relieved we were in one piece, and we spent Diwali and Christmas with them having such a good time. We visited more relatives, and Mum was shopping endlessly for the grandchildren and family in England.

Making papad with Tejal, Rukhimami, Tara, Mum and cousin Jagu in Aradhana

Janet had an emotional phone call from her family on Christmas Day – it was the first time she heard their voices in three months. Her sheer joy and emotion at speaking to them, made my Indian family aware how we all have close bonds. They had heard that white families in England were not close like us. It was an interesting reminder about how stereotypes are perpetuated on all sides. Many Asian communities came to England believing that white families just let their children leave home because they had no real bonds as a family unit. The irony was that Janet's mother's side had wide extended relationships with grandparents, aunts, uncles and cousins and shared love and commitment.

My most memorable moment was visiting my Jiviphoi, my dad's sister.

Our last visit to see Jiviphoi with Tara and Mum

She was so happy to see us but worried that I was not married and that I was wearing plastic earrings instead of gold. She was tiny and frail now and all alone. We said our final farewell knowing we would never see her again. The old men and women who were on their own near the end of their lives in little villages, many of whom were close relatives of ours, really haunted us. Mum and I talk a lot about their loneliness and isolation at the end of their lives.

My Mum and I prepared our bags for the journey home on New Year's Eve. It was very emotional leaving my extended family. I felt so reconnected to them. We all cried and said our farewells, receiving blessings and garlands with prayers for safe travels as are the usual Hindu rituals for travelling overseas. At Bombay Airport, Mum and I said farewell to Janet too as she was staying in Bangalore for a month extra to do her planned placement. I think at that moment we both so wished she was coming back with us. We had spent three intense months together and it just felt wrong to leave her in India without us. It was a wrench, but Janet bravely stayed on and did some interesting work.

The stay with my family and our travels had a profound effect on me and Janet. It really helped me clarify my sense of identity and embrace my Indian side. Reconnecting with my family and feeling valued by them as an independent woman was the most reassuring aspect for me. Migration and my western education had not created the massive chasm that I had feared. I realised those five and a half years in India before we moved to England had a truly valuable impact on my brothers and I, even though we had become British Asians now.

As a result of that trip, we saw Janet become a phoi (aunt, equivalent to father's sister…it gets complicated so check the glossary) to my nieces and nephews and a familiar name in our household in Leicester and Gujarat. Likewise, years later now that we have families of our own, she is a 'Masi' to my two daughters and I am 'Aunty' to her two daughters. She is the 'sister' I never had and a loyal friend. She and I are still close friends after 45 years and involved in joint family events – births, deaths, marriages and there are regular visits between Bristol and Cornwall.

Settling in Bristol

On returning after the India trip, I settled down to the rhythm of life in Bristol. I enjoyed my job with its challenges but also opportunities to work in creative ways. The great surprise when I got back was that Peter had managed to get tickets for the Live Aid concert at Wembley, which was at that time an exciting venture in fundraising for the relief of the famine taking place in Ethiopia. There are many schools of thought about the ethics of this approach nowadays, but at the time it was a practical response to something that was hard to watch on our TV news by a range of musicians and driven by Bob Geldof. We went to London Wembley Stadium on 13th July 1985 and saw an incredible concert amongst 72,000 other people. A concert was also taking place at the John F Kennedy stadium in Philadelphia USA with 89,000 in attendance. The concerts were then beamed across 150 countries using military satellites and raised £40m on the day; the trust has subsequently raised over £140m over the last 40 years.

In July 1982, I had been appointed as the first Black/Asian Probation Officer by the Avon Probation Service and was interviewed by BBC Radio Bristol on my early experience. I went on to do interesting and innovative work with women in the probation service, using a feminist groupwork approach, which was later published in an academic journal. Also, with my union NAPO (National Association of Probation Officers) and 'Women in NAPO' we campaigned to decriminalise prostitution offences. We made a case to our courts as probation officers for an 'absolute discharge' recommendation for women who had been charged with prostitution. We made an economic case as to why they should not get any other form of sentencing including fines. We had regular meetings with the magistrates' committee and were able to influence some aspects of local policy then, in a way I cannot believe officers would be able to do in the present political climate. I was also highly active in the racism and antiracism work in Bristol and helped organise one of the first conferences called 'Ethnic sensitivity to social work practice'. It was early days we were finding our way!

This was the first of many collaborative partnerships I helped to establish to encourage discussion and to develop good policy and practice in social work in Bristol across local authority workers, the higher education institutions training social workers and probation officers, and the voluntary sector. That first conference was chaired by Reena Bhavnani (founder of Southall Black Sisters and later a well-respected anti-racist activist who moved to London and sadly died in 2008). It also brought me into contact with Allan Brown, who was a social work academic at Bristol University. He was very influential in the field of 'Groupwork' in social work and published many social work textbooks. Many of us who were interested in a social action approach to social work and work with offenders (where individualised practice was not the only focus) found Allan's books on theory and skills in 'Groupwork' very exciting and helpful as students and later as professional practitioners in a variety of social work settings.

Meanwhile I developed my knowledge and experience as a practice teacher, training students. My work on the National Training Committee on NAPO was valuable. In addition, I helped teach on the Bristol University groupwork skills programme because of my work with women offenders. Later this enabled me to apply for a position as a lecturer in social work at Bristol University in January 1988.

Staff photo of Tara on appointment as a lecturer in Social Work at the University of Bristol

Initially this was on a two year secondment from the Probation Service. This gave me more opportunities to develop and apply my interest in policy and practice in anti-discrimination but also opportunities for research and collaboration, both nationally and internationally. As a recent practitioner, teaching on the Probation option and skills-based work was a positive experience in an academic setting. I worked closely with Allan, and we wrote joint articles and presented papers at international conferences. We co-edited a book (Race and Groupwork) encouraging social work practitioners using groupwork approaches with a race dimension to write about it. The book helped them to articulate their 'practice theories' rather than just rely on academically driven theories. Allan was also the editor of the international peer reviewed journal, 'Groupwork'. When he retired, I was one of three women who became co-editors, along with a colleague based in Ireland and Claire from Leicester. This provided a broader spectrum of editorial interests and involvement.

Outside work, I was still heavily involved in the Labour Party and at the 1985 Conference I tried to speak at the Black Sections debate to which I wore a sari to show solidarity with all non-white delegates. There was a move by the Labour leadership to divide the Asian and African Caribbean delegates in respect of the conference resolution on setting up of 'Black Sections', so it was important for us to be seen to be united. There were other delegates there such as Diane Abbott (who later became the first Black woman Labour MP) and Linda Bellos (a prominent Black Labour Party activist working in Lambeth). I felt compelled to challenge the chair as not many of us were selected to speak in favour of the Black Section motion. I made my way to the rostrum to lay my challenge, but the microphone was cut off. The BBC picked up my protest on their microphone and my poor Mum in Leicester doing her vacuuming with the TV on, saw her daughter being asked to leave the rostrum while still protesting. Mum knew I was trying to get my voice heard but was wondering why I had a sari on! Generally, I only wore a sari for official occasions. Next day, in the Bristol Evening Post there was front page headline 'The Black Rage of Tara'.

I later became the Chair of Bristol East Constituency and Peter was the Secretary. I continued my involvement with Brislington Labour Women's Section and Bristol Labour Women's Council. We were both encouraged to think about going for selection to be parliamentary candidates or councillors at different stages of our political activism but neither of us were interested in that path, believing our efforts were better served in supporting good candidates and servicing the branches and the constituency. We supported and worked for candidates who were selected either as councillors or parliamentary candidates during most of our time in the Party. Our lives were consumed by party politics, attending meetings, writing newsletters, and campaigning alongside wider activism that stemmed from it. Around this time the campaign against the Poll Tax was a huge challenge to the Tory Government and we were all committed at local and national level to fight against it. Much of this 'Can't Pay, Won't Pay' campaign was organised outside the Labour Party. Meanwhile we were increasingly unhappy with many policy decisions by the Labour Party and much of our activism by now was outside the Party. The final straw was in 1991, and we left the Labour Party over its position on the First Gulf War.

In 2016, I rejoined after another election defeat for Labour. For a few years I was even encouraged to be active again and became a Branch Chair but left again around 2023. I was disillusioned by the continued attacks on the left of the party and recognised that the membership and the constituencies had even less power to influence policy directions than we had earlier. The centrally controlled agenda has stripped any activism and become a machine to manipulate desired candidates for selection at local and national level, and to discipline anyone not in agreement with the party line and prevent meaningful debate.

Peter and I lived together in my Bristol house after he came to Leicester to meet the family. Neither of us were sold on marriage as an institution but had made a commitment to each other. I introduced Peter to my family with Janet acting as his 'partner' in case relatives should pop round while he was there. On reflection, it was funny, as Janet left early, and my aunt did 'pop in'. We scrambled Peter out of the back door so they would not catch on that I had brought a white man to meet my family. It was not as we planned. Suresh was really upset for Peter and for me, it helped me to decide that getting married would give us legitimacy as a couple in the eyes of our community. By then my family had moved on from the scenario of an arranged marriage, so getting married to a white man was a compromise I felt I could make. Mum even said we could just pretend to be married as she knew I was opposed to marriage as an institution (although I'm not sure if that evermade sense to Mum). The important thing was that she was now just thinking about me and my happiness, rather than how we would be seen by other people. That seemed such amazing progress.

We had a small wedding at our house in Bristol with Peter's family and mine and some friends. Janet came to help me set up, and my family with my nieces and nephews dressed in colourful Indian outfits came on the day. I did not wear the wonderful jewellery and wedding adornments that Mum had bought from India as it was not that kind of a wedding. I did buy myself a new sari fit for a wedding and Mum paid for a suit for Peter (as a nod to our tradition). Janet also wore a sari. Mum made the food aided by Sumitra and Suresh. I know that bringing the food and cooking was stressful as it was made the night before in Leicester and had to be ferried in two cars full of people with limited boot space. But Peter's family loved it as did friends who were invited. They still talk about it.

There was an evening party at Transport House in Bristol (Transport and General Workers Union building, now Unite's Tony Benn House). The venue was not great for a party, but lots of our friends from the Labour Party and colleagues from work came along and we had a good time. The next day Peter and I went to see U2's Joshua Tree concert at Cardiff and then on the Monday we went to work. The reason we did not have any time off work was because Peter had used up all his holidays for the General Election campaign earlier in March of 1987.

I was still on the 2-year secondment at Bristol University when a full-time tenured appointment came up under the 'New Blood Scheme' predominantly teaching on the probation option. I was pregnant with my first child by then, and I was not sure I wanted a full-time post at the time. I invited my friend and colleague, Hilary Burgess, who was already teaching at the university, to join me in a job-share application. We were the first pair to apply and get a job-share post at the University. My friendship with Hilary, is another one that transcends four decades, along with another colleague and friend, Margaret Boushel, who worked alongside us in the social work department, teaching on 'Children and Families'.

From home to seeking asro at ASRA

Back in Leicester Mum lived with Suresh, Sumitra, and by now their three children. Chandra and his growing family, also with three children, were visiting Leicester regularly at weekends. I was single for some years and doing what aunts do which was to dote on my nieces and nephews and play with them. Mum was trying to do what a traditional Indian mum and grandmother did, which was to feed everyone, help maintain the home and look after the grandchildren. Slowly over the years tensions began to build. On the weekends when both Chandra, Pat and family and I came it was full-on cooking and preparing food for Mum and to a degree Sumitra. Pressure and tensions started to build up in hosting and cooking and providing food. The role of providing food somehow got amplified to such a degree that the family gatherings, although sometimes great, were at other times quite strained. There was mounting underlying conflict between Mum and my sister-in-law. Despite Mum helping to 'service' the home, the children and the wider relationship with our community, the tension worsened; my brother was caught in between, trying to be supportive to both. In the early days, when their first daughter was about two, they went to India on holiday while Mum looked after their daughter (I took time off work to help too). So, there were obvious benefits to my Mum's presence in the home, and more so after the other two children were born.

By then I had my first child – a daughter. I remember finding out that I was pregnant with my second child and going to Leicester to share our good news, but my Mum had her bag packed to come back with us to Bristol as they needed some respite from each other. We were not expecting that and took my Mum home with us for a week or so. Before then Mum had been to India for six months again to give them time on their own, but it was not enough, and it was clear that Mum would have to leave the house. In some ways this was not dissimilar from dynamics in other families both in India and in those that had settled in western countries. One could argue it was natural progression in all societies, but the nature of the extended family was changing in professional and middle-class families in some Asian communities (like ours) more than others. I went to observe some of the changes taking place in families in Gujarat, India, as part of my academic research in the early 1990's and found that garda ghar (older people's homes) provision was emerging within a range of communities in India itself. Many I observed over in Gujarat were rather basic dormitories but the fact that they were opening to care for older people outside the family home was a revelation.

In Britain, there was the recurring issue of education and opportunities for Asian women which began to have a real impact. Some young couples who had careers were working away so could live away from their 'in-laws' legitimately and without judgement. Similarly, as they got older, grandchildren could not easily reconcile themselves to traditional expectations placed on them, although many did retain a sense of respect for older relatives. Often the small houses made it hard to accommodate growing families, and overcrowding added to the tensions of catering for the needs of both younger and older generations. Often, the daughters-in-law were working outside the home too, so there was an expectation to live a more independent life. The values of the families wanting to have space and a quality of life that they perceived others had, without the obligation to live with parents-in-law, started to have an impact more widely. In my family's case the space was also a factor. The house only had three bedrooms, and the box room was literally just that so made the situation more difficult as the children were growing. I also felt Bhabhi's perception was that Chandra and my family life away from Leicester was easier and 'freer.' Although totally untrue - we had no childcare support and I juggled a demanding career with all the daily responsibilities as Peter was often working abroad, I can appreciate that perception. In addition, Mum's role as a widowed mother living with her eldest son meant the weight of servicing Chandra and later my family on our visits fell on Suresh's household. This was made worse by the fact that we all lived outside Leicester, so our visits necessitated staying over 1-2 nights in a very overcrowded house. Had we all lived in Leicester it may have been easier. In those days people did not stay in hotels or Airbnb when visiting, whereas nowadays that is more of an option and considered acceptable with families without judgement about lack of hospitality from an older brother's household.

There followed a challenging period for Mum as she had become homeless, and she lived in a hostel for about six months in an area of Leicester that was unfamiliar and daunting. The light at the end of that tunnel was that she was given a flat in new-build supported housing accommodation run by ASRA Housing Association. Undoubtedly, it was a dispiriting time for her, and the sense of abandonment was palpable. I am sure she must have wondered if this would ever have happened if my Dad had lived. It was another punishment of widowhood, as she saw it. However, the fact that these types of accommodation were available in Leicester does indicate that there was a demand within the Asian communities. It was fortunate that since Leicester had a large Asian population some of the needs of the older generation began to be met in a very practical way. In Gujarati to give asro is to give support.

Jaffer Kapasi recalls in 'Belgrave Memories 1945-2005' (Bill Law & Tim Haq) that he came across an incident where an Indian woman was sleeping in the garage of her son and daughter-in-law's house. A white neighbour reported this to social services who became involved. Soon they realised that the need for a Housing Association to provide housing for the Asian older people was becoming more urgent. ASRA was developed because of this. In terms of culture, language, residents and staff it was very much geared to Asian communities in general. As well as this new facility there was also Gandhi House, but usually this was full.

When Mum eventually got a place in this new-build she was one of the first residents. Although it felt strange and upsetting to all of us for a long time, it was to be her new home, and she would eventually learn to love her private space. Suresh worked extremely hard to secure her accommodation as quickly as possible. Coincidently, my Ajima died about the time Mum moved to the flat. She was very upset to lose Ajima but also relieved that she died without suffering too long with ill health and not having to understand her daughter's predicament. My Ajima would have been devastated to know her eldest daughter had to leave her family home. It was amazing how Mum's faith helped her to establish an independent life at the same time as coping with losing her mother - who was also her close friend and confidant.

My Mum was living alone by the time my youngest was one year old, so our visits were based in Mum's flat. As my daughters were the youngest cohort of grandchildren, they always saw the Leicester base as 'Ma's place'. As time wore on, we all gravitated to Mum's little flat, as that became her permanent home. The Braunstone home was no longer our family base. From this point, our 'traditional' roles and relationships as a Prajapati family changed and reshaped slowly over the coming years. Mum's move to her independent flat meant Bhabhi could assert her role as the head of her own household; in effect this meant that she and Suresh were no longer head of the wider household in a traditional sense. Our family were all now independent household units bound together by Mum. To some extent, Chandra and I were already independent in how we lived because of the marriage choices we had made outside our jati although we kept our cultural and Prajapati connections via the Leicester family base, our kutumb. But with Mum having to move out of the communal family home with her eldest son and his family, the centrality of their joint roles was broken both symbolically and emotionally. Suresh and Mum were still a point of reference for our Prajapati news and events in Leicester and with the diaspora, as well as links with our relatives in India. Both Chandra and I respect the role of our eldest brother, and he is still our representative of the family especially as Mum gets much older. Although I refer to Suresh and Chandra by name in this book, personally I will always refer to them as Bhai (although using their names with the suffix bhai to difference them) as a sign of respect for my older brothers. Chandra will always refer to Suresh as Bhai too as he is younger.

Over the years, we saw many individuals move to Mum's accommodation seeking asro from other cities where facilities like this did not exist. The development is situated in St Mathew's estate, which is the one we all feared as we were growing up, as it was a white racist area in the 1970's. It has changed to an area that accommodates refugees, asylum seekers and migrants, and borders onto the Belgrave area, which is very familiar to my

Mum and indeed our old neighbourhood. 'The Golden Mile' is a bustling area with sari shops, gold shops, restaurants of different specialities and street food and sweetmeat and savoury delicacies. Asian people come from all over England for shopping and especially for wedding purchases. It is now a tourist hot-spot too and Leicester City Council promotes it as such. People come for city breaks especially at the Diwali festival. The famous Belgrave Neighbourhood Centre where community activities take place is situated here and has been a feature since 1977. It was previously Belgrave Hall Wesleyan Methodist Church and Mantle Memorial School. The City Council took over the empty buildings and created the neighbourhood centre. I remember this as I was in Leicester between finishing university and my job in Manchester when it opened, and I explored the possibility of finding a community work role. This is where Mum first started to attend Swadhya.

My Mum adopted the religious avenue of the Swadhya Movement to find a way of expanding her horizons. Swadhya is not so much focussed on temples and rituals but focusses more on self-study, growth, and service within the religious framework of Hinduism. Dada was the spiritual leader, and Mum was really inspired by the message when she joined the group in her mid-forties. Suresh used to give her lifts to the centre and later when they moved to Braunstone he would wait at the back of Belgrave Neighbourhood Centre, so he would not have to make two trips. He began to feel motivated to join and started to help promote Dada's pravachans (inspiring sermons) through his skills in media and technology. These pravachans were later shared in large venues in places like Leicester and London. Mum attended them and did regular bhakti pheri (visiting other cities to spread the message). Once living away from the family, she got a lot of strength from this. It helped to make my Mum more of an independent thinker and she began to voice her opinions more clearly to us. She would talk about wider philosophical things, including the Swadhya movement being a 'social force'. She often likened it to my work in social work and enabling people to find a voice. The people she met inspired her and her approach to her life changed. She was able to go on group travels around the country and to parts of Europe. Swadhya was very influential in the lives of both my Mum and Suresh, and they were involved for over thirty years. They are no longer active members, but it is still Mum's faith, and it helps her navigate her life.

At Mum's flat to attend Navratri celebrations in Leicester so we are dressed up. Left to right: Mum, Tara, Sunita and Nalini

She was 58 years old when she moved to ASRA supported housing and had a long life still to live. The flat is on the first floor but for years she took over a few raised square containers on the ground floor garden area, which originally had plant displays. Over a period, they had become neglected, and Mum worked her way to develop three raised beds, growing spinach, garlic, onions, potatoes, beans, coriander and chillis. With spinach leaves she made lots of patra (vegetarian spiced rolls) for us, and many curries from a few French bean plants that my friend Sharon gave her. It was utterly amazing to see her grow things very simply. She also made do with cast-off bits that she found abandoned in the street; the most impressive was her water butt find and the way she put it together in the garden. She would find use for a lot of discarded plastic. It was not a fancy garden and more like an allotment. Those early days at Munsad had given her the confidence to have a go as she was remarkably familiar with growing vegetables. It was a dramatic transition for Mum, and for us it was a great consolation to see her rebuilding her life and thriving.

As well as cultivating her raised beds and making us delicious food from her garden, she hosted visits from her family from India. Her two brothers (Manekmama and Kishormama) came with their wives on two separate occasions, and they were able to stay in the guest room at the complex and Mum hosted them brilliantly in her small flat. Her widowed sister-in-law (Rukhimami) visited from India too and again Mum looked after her and they were reassured that she was happy. My brothers and I and our families have all been fed on chicken sak, lamb/vegetable biriyanis, dahls, kaman, bhat - dahl, kitchri with kadhi, a variety of pulses and vegetables, papad, pickle, idli, paratha, pooras, bhajias, samosas, chutneys, dhokri, and keema. Sweet dishes include ladoo, ras/puri, siro, dudh pak, mithai, khajli, gugra and jalebis. There are too many dishes to list, and we all have our favourites - not to mention millions of rotlis she must have fed us and given to us to take home. Of course, part of my mum's signature cuisine is her blend of garam masala and dhana/jeeru spice mixes so loved in Gujarati cooking. All of us have jars of it and even the grandchildren in Bristol have it as a store cupboard ingredient.

Mum in her garden

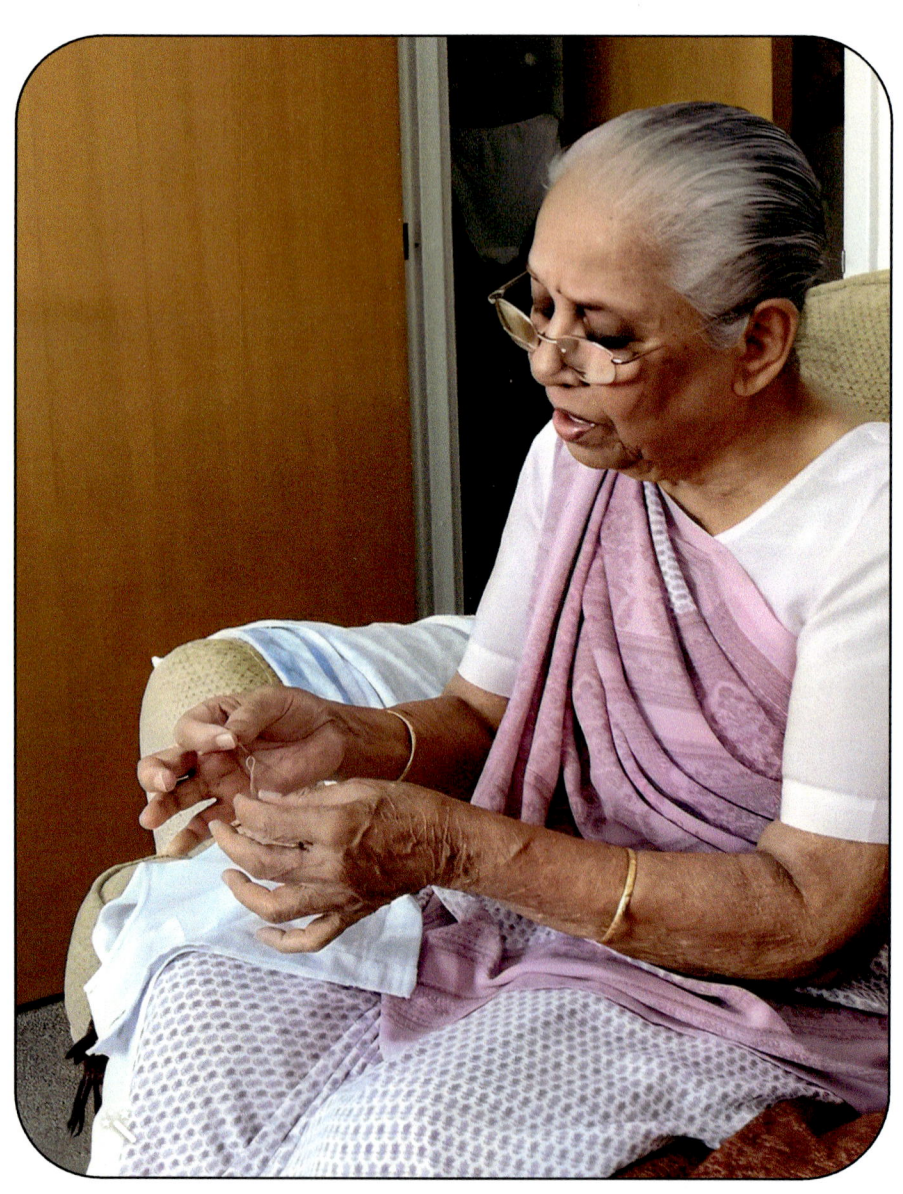

Mum embroidering in her flat

Like a lot of warden-controlled Housing Association developments, ASRA no longer has that aspect of support and over the years different companies have taken over the complex. It has been opened out to non-Asian residents in recent years as the demand for housing is ever increasing. Mum is one of the original residents still there, aged over ninety at the time of writing. Over 25 residents have died over the period of her tenancy, not surprising when they are older people, although thankfully no one died from Covid-19 in the pandemic. She has lost a couple of close friends but accepts that loss is a natural part of life's experiences, especially in an older people's residence. Mum has had continuous residency of 33 years in this accommodation, for which she is happy and grateful. This is a genuine feeling because when I phone her, she talks very proudly of living there, rather than with any of the family. She knows it gives her freedom to do what she likes without worrying about fitting in with other people's plans. When she arrived, it was the first time in her life she not only had 'a room of her own' but a place of her own. The ordeal of losing her family home was the most challenging time of her life, and something that was painful for an exceptionally long time. It was the loss of her way of life and the roles she had held, and she was frightened by the unfamiliar change in her life. The loss of her previous home was also a loss of identity. In her new home however, she forged a new role and regained her identity, status and indeed gravitas within the Prajapati community. Over the years many relatives are envious of her life and independence. In time, it was to prove to be the most liberating start to the rest of her new life. She would not change it now for anything. She has space and yet people around her and all the family come and go and keep in touch through variety of means. In her 90's she also values the flat for its accessibility and the lack of trip hazards she might have encountered elsewhere. All that is important, and it means she does not need to relocate or move and can live independently as long as possible.

Health and reframing Mum's life

Healthwise, it has not been plain sailing for my mother. She was 69 when she started to feel ill and lose weight. Eventually she was diagnosed with bowel cancer. Initially, her operation went well, and the surgeon was happy. She was due to go home, went to have a shower but swiftly became very poorly with the hospital-acquired infection Clostridium Difficile (C.Diff). Suddenly she was extremely ill post-operatively. This led to another major challenge in her life.

C.Diff was rife in hospitals at the time and many older people died. It causes non-stop diarrhoea and weakness from lack of food and dehydration. Suresh, Sumitra and Chandra were around, and I left the children for periods of time in Bristol with Peter to help. It was difficult as he was working full time and travelling. I had to cancel extensive freelance projects, but I wanted to be near Mum, so Peter and the children supported me fully. Even in those days the system seemed stretched, and Sumitra and I undertook shifts at the hospital. Not being able to go back to my own house and family after emotional days at hospital was difficult. I went to and from Leicester and Bristol frequently, and it was a relief to see my daughters (14 and 12 years old at the time) and Peter – and I know it was hard for them too. Night shifts with Mum gave me a different insight into the hospital. Doctors and staff were generally incredibly good but observing different nurses on shift as a relative – as opposed to a patient – was an eye-opener. I had been a patient in hospital on numerous occasions for serious health issues and recognised that Mum was extremely ill and could not speak for herself. She had all of us around her but felt powerless if we were not there. Luckily, she turned a corner just as we had given up hope. The nutritionist's intervention worked.

She regained her strength slowly and made steady progress over a period of weeks. Later she had to have more surgery in relation to the bowel cancer; on this occasion she was on a general ward in a different hospital. This time her wounds took longer to heal. Once again, she felt very unhappy in the hospital setting. I found her care to be variable depending on the nurses taking care of her. One day I took her some hot kitchri (lentil and rice dish) from a restaurant only to be told she had been designated as 'nil by mouth'. I asked why and they did not know. Poor Mum could smell the kitchri and was not allowed to eat it. I later found out she should not have been designated as 'nil by mouth' and could have eaten it. She was very hungry. The nurses were not vigilant and incidents like this eroded her confidence in the way they cared for her. Her lack of English and ability to communicate added to her feeling of vulnerability. This variation in care depending on which nursing staff was on duty is a theme I had experienced myself many times as a patient and particularly so after serious brain surgery in Cambridge I had some years later. This seemed to stem in part from the pressures in the system, but it also showed that there were not consistent standards across nursing staff and grades. There is also an important discussion going on in the health service about the use of registered and non-registered health professionals in the mix. I am a great advocate of the NHS and defender of the enshrined values, but I felt the often excellent surgical interventions were not always backed up by quality, consistent nursing care unless you were in intensive care. As a Non-Executive Director/Vice Chair/Chair and champion of Patient Public Involvement in Health Trusts for over 25 years, I was constantly raising issues of listening to patients and improving their experience. It is a wider issue of workforce planning, not enough staffing, lack of training and lack of support for staff too. As a patient it can feel like a very lonely place. However, all these shortcomings can be remedied, and I hope they will be in time.

Mum seemed to get better as time went on but when confronted with an option to have more treatment in the form of chemotherapy, she stood firm. She did not want any further treatment or interventions that might lead to hospitalisation. She would take her chances. She reclaimed the power to direct her own life for however long she had left.

She was clear she was going to live the rest of her life on her own terms. She felt she had already lived a long life and was well over 70 by now. Most of our relatives died young, so felt she had been blessed so far. She had her faith and learning from Swadhya and was going to live her life with renewed commitment to each day. She decided to reframe the rest of her life as a 'new life', echoing the words of that early TV programme 'Naya Jeevan, Naya Zindagi' (New Way, New Life). She decided to unburden herself from the shackles of the past and not hold negative thoughts and feelings about anyone. It is fair to say that her ability to stay true to that philosophy has certainly changed all our relationships with her.

She gave up being at all judgemental about her children, her family and siblings, family and friends.

In writing this social history/memoir I have rewritten much about my mother's relationship with me (and mine with her) because of her very positive 'reframing' of her life going forward. I think this was a watershed moment for Mum and our 'mother-daughter relationship'. Whilst there had been other turning points that I have already covered, this was dramatic and transformative. From my point of view, it meant she could embrace us all for who we all were and what we had achieved, and to see achievements, not in a way of wealth, fame, fortune or status but in terms of getting on with life in the way we choose to live it. She values people differently now. My earlier relationship with my Mum was marred by all sorts of judgments she made about me and my choices in life. The clear gendered approach to handling her children was as much about the cultural context of our life as well as her own experiences. But this reframing encapsulates the transformation she underwent both for herself and in and her relationships with all. We are all so much older and we all have our own children and grandchildren so there is much to learn about each other as my brothers and I embark on the next stage of our lives.

Writing this memoir has changed how I see my mother, and the immense hurt I felt at times growing up (shared by many daughters I know who feel like this about their mothers whatever the cultural context) has dissipated. Having my own children has helped me to understand things better too and seeing how proud she is of me, my brothers and our families, including each one of her grandchildren. Her life and achievements are valued through seeing her family and all their offspring living a meaningful life however we choose to define meaningful. Fitting in or succeeding as society determines is less of a concern now for Mum, who cares more about being ethical and doing your best. To some extent she has always had these beliefs, but they are much clearer. She is optimistic that the great grandchildren will have as good a life as possible, although she knows that she has no idea what that will entail. The years since moving to the flat have been a transformative journey for her. Like me she has used writing as a way of processing her life and trying to understand it better. It is amazing to think she had hardly any education, but writing (and reading) has been her therapeutic tool. In the post-surgery years, she has not only survived but since refusing further treatment has taken control of her life and lived it with vigour, wisdom and humility.

I believe that the last twenty-one years, have for her been an exemplar of that philosophy, and a life well lived. Mum made peace with Desh and said her goodbyes when I took her to the double wedding of her two nieces in 2009. My Ajima died over thirty years ago but had been able to visit us in England before her death, so she was able to see her daughters and families.

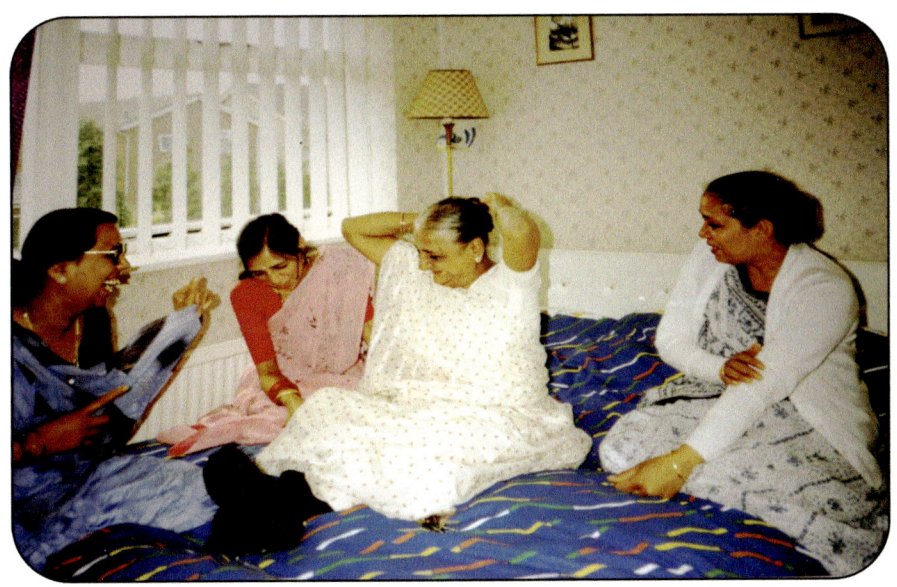

Ajima's visit to England. Captured is a joyous moment with her daughters. Left to right: Padmamasi, Ramilamasi, Ajima and Mum

My mamas (her brothers Manek and Kishor) are still alive in India, and both have spent time with their eldest sister in England in recent years. Modern technology allows them to see each other and talk on the phone. My Mum's two sisters and their families live in Leicester and Rugby, and they stay connected. Sadly, Padmamasi died in Leicester in November

2024. We all attended the funeral, reconnecting and remembering the early days with our cousins in Leicester.

To some extent, our family and extended family are a classic example of adaptation to a new world with our children, grandchildren and great grandchildren. Chandra and I still see and treat Suresh as our older brother deserving of the respect bestowed on an older brother, which is very important to our values and how we were raised. This has been reinforced as my Mum has aged and needs more practical support. Suresh provides that, partly because he lives nearby, but partly because he is doing what older sons have done in our Prajapati community - that is to care for his parent. Chandra and I also play an important role in Mum's life, but there is a strong and vital reassurance for us that Suresh is nearby. Chandra also provides an important role with his medical oversight for mum; and indeed for all of us as we need his expertise from time to time!

Mum feels she is blessed compared to older relatives who were left behind in the villages and towns when families like ours migrated. Like all older people she wants to stay independent in her home. All families go through ups and down and we certainly have done so. Mum has been relatively lucky to stay in good health despite her past cancer experience.

Is it luck, good genes, is it her newfound philosophy, her diet of healthy home-made food and no alcohol or her faith and an innovative approach to life that enable her to thrive? We do not know, but we do know she is as happy and contended as you can be at 91 years of age. That happiness she says, comes from the family and family relationships and from the community. Our Prajapati Gujarati community (whether hailing from India or East Africa to arrive in England) has changed tremendously, but religion, culture, food, and festivals all still play a big part for many of us. Within our family our religious faiths range from atheist, agnostic, Jewish, Hindu and Catholic – and possibly other faiths too. But we still observe many of the festivals in our Hindu calendar, not because we are all religious or Hindus, but they are seen more as cultural practices through which we can celebrate our identity and heritage. Our children are keen to preserve their family traditions too. Food, clothes, music and dance are part of preserving the identity, even if it is less 'pure' and more of a 'fusion'. Furthermore, in recent years we now have a global migration of people from all over the world including more Gujarati people from former Portuguese colonies such as Daman and Dui, and other areas of India.

In addition, people from Europe, Somalia, Syria, Sudan, Afghanistan, Iraq, Hong Kong, Ukraine have migrated to the UK, and others have arrived as refugees and asylum seekers from all over the world. They have added to the tapestry of a new Britain and its earlier post-war settlers. However, political shifts are taking place worldwide and there is no certainty for new migrants in how their life will shape and evolve here. There is greater hostility to their presence especially if they are 'people of colour' and from poorer nations. Refuge and asylum – those words have lost their original meaning and now equated to 'illegal migration'. I fear governments of all hues are fixated by a dangerous rhetoric – xenophobia and protectionism clouds judgements and there is a backlash that makes us all fearful.

All migrants face their own challenges in the ever-changing face of Britain. We have been in this country well over sixty years and feel we have settled here. We have contributed enormously through our work and as citizens in all walks of life. Our family is multi-racial, and our children do not all speak Gujarati. The ones that did grow up with my Mum in Leicester all communicate in Gujarati with varying degree of fluency. They are lucky to have that early childhood with Mum. Neither Chandra's nor my children grew up with Gujarati spoken in our households as our partners were not Gujarati speakers. My daughters cannot speak to their Ajima in Gujarati, and she still does not speak English. Gestures, and translation from me help my daughters to relate to Mum, but it means nuances sometimes 'get lost' in translation. I often felt sad about this but came across this letter my eldest daughter had written for my Mum's 80th Birthday. She had asked me to translate it to her Ajima (my daughters, Nalini and Sunita, have always called her Ma as do all my nieces and nephews) and I had kept her beautifully handwritten copy. I have reproduced it below as a way of ending this journey because it reassured me that Mum's legacy is intact, and language is not a barrier if we share our stories and make ourselves understood by our actions, sharing food, our heritage and history, attending festivals and all the things my daughters have enjoyed and participated in with my Indian family over their life. They are anxious to continue to participate in future with their children – the next generation.

With subsequent generations we will all struggle to 'be understood', and even with one language there will be challenges to interpreting the ever-changing world, our knowledge and experiences. I am sure if my daughters were ever to write a memoir there may be similar themes, with dimensions of their dual heritage which is unique to them.

Dear Ma

HAPPY 80th BIRTHDAY!!!!

You look so Beautiful and so young Ma! I can only hope I have your genes!

As I write this, Mum is telling me about how you like to write. She also tells me that you love to read and so I have got you a subscription for Garvi Gujarat. I hope you like it. Mum says you read your friend's copy. Now you have your own.

I love that you write. I know Mum does (and I do too). I even think Sunita does a bit – Even more reason as to why I think I am in the running for good genes!

As my mum writes, she tells stories of you moving from India. My mum is so good at informing us of what you went through. I hope you don't think I am ignorant to the facts. I am so proud of what you have done and in awe and amazed. I cannot imagine but all I can say is the bravery and sacrifices you made have in turn made us who we are today. My Grandmothers have shown me that to be strong we have to learn and cope with change.

My mum and dad have brought me and Sunita up well. With the knowledge of what our families and especially the women in our families have achieved. They have taught us our history and because of that we are well equipped for the future.

You have shown bravery, kindness and acceptance. I can only hope that when I am 80, I will look back and tell extraordinary stories too. You have taught us to be true to ourselves and culturally aware of our heritage and be open and adapt to new things. My mum and dad have enforced this message.

I hope I have even half of your courage in life. I want you to know that I love you loads and so grateful for all you and our family have done.

I hope you are happy and wish you only that on your birthday and for many more to come.

All my love

Nalini xxx

Overleaf: Family group at Mum's 90th birthday

Glossary

Prajapati - is a multifaceted term with origins in Sanskrit. It is a Vedic deity in Hinduism often associated with creation and reproduction. Hindus associate it with a caste/jati of kumbhars (potters), carpenters, tailors, generally skilled crafts and increasingly professional people. My family and our wider family would all see themselves as Prajapatis and indeed the Shree Prajapati Association (UK) is a national and international organisation with membership drawn from the caste/jati members across the diaspora.

Basic family relationship and terms used by Prajapatis:

Ajima – Maternal grandmother.

Ajabapa – Maternal grandfather.

Ba – Mother/Mum.

Bapuji – Father/Dad.

Bapa – Grandad or generic term for older male relatives/family friends. Can be used on both maternal and paternal side. We used it for many of our uncles (Kakas), for example my dad's brother Chagan, we always called Chagan Bapa and his wife Nani Ma; Bhuli Ma in India was her sister, married to my dad's brother and technically Kaki.

Ben – Sister. Often used at the end of a female name but older sister often referred to as Ben as a sign of respect (e.g. Laxmi Ben but also just 'Ben' when addressed by her younger siblings or relatives). Ben also used generically to address women. Our cousin (Dad's Niece) would be termed 'Bhani Ben' (cousin-sister) to denote the close blood relation tie to differentiate from distant cousins.

Bhai – Brother. Often used at the end of a male name as sign of respect, but older brothers are usually referred to as Bhai (e.g. Suresh Bhai, Chandrakant Bhai or just Bhai when addressed by younger siblings or relatives). Bhai is also used generically to address men. Our cousin (Dad's nephew) would be termed 'Balwant Bhai' (cousin- brother) to denote the close blood relation tie and to differentiate from distant cousins.

Bhabhi – Wife of brother. For example, Suresh's wife Sumitra is my Bhabhi. Also generically used to refer to partner or wife of anyone regarded or called Bhai. For example, in our early days in Leicester our lodgers were Dullabh Bhai and his wife Dhai Bhabhi.

Dada – Paternal grandfather (in our case Makan Dada but we never knew him so not a term we used). We refer to him as Makan Bapa (see Bapa) – a term used widely in our family for those who are older (in age or hierarchy) in the family.

Dadi (Ma) – Paternal Grandmother. In our case Ladu but we tended to call her Ladu Ma rather than Dadi. Ma is traditionally used for grandmother or older aunts (e.g. Bhulima) in our family who are older or more senior in the family.

Kaka – Father's brother, or if a younger uncle sometimes called Nana. Also used for male relatives who are friends or relations from father's side. Technically Chagan Bhai, our Dad's brother, should be Kaka, but as he was older than Dad and our paternal grandfather had died, we referred to him as Bapa (see Bapa) – considered more respectful for a senior figure.

Kaki – Father's sister-in-law (if married to younger uncle) sometimes called Nani. Also used for partner and spouse of male relatives or friends from Dad's side. Technically Bhuli Ben who is a widowed aunt and my Dad's sister-in-law should be Bhuli Kaki but again as she was older in the hierarchy, she was known to us as Bhuli Ma (See Ma) – considered more respectful for senior figure.

Ma – Grandmother or generic term for older female relatives or family friends. Can be used on both maternal and paternal side. Even older aunts are called Ma. For example, Diwali Ma (was technically a Kaki). Again, to do with age and degree of seniority.

Mama – Mother's brother. Also used to refer to male relatives, cousins, or friends on mother's side. Our Mama's are all my mum's brothers and her male cousins.

Mami – Mother's sister-in-law, married to Mama. Also used to refer to partners and wives of male relatives, cousins, friends on mother's side.

Masi – Mother's sister. Also used widely for mother's close friendships. Masi is also used to refer generically to older women. I don't have a sister, but my cousin Bhaniben's children will call me Masi as close 'cousin-sister' are treated almost as siblings.

Masa – Mother's brother-in-law, usually married to Masi.

Phoi – Father's sister (in our case Jivi Phoi). Also used for close female relations associated with Father, for example 'cousin-sister' (see Ben) or just cousins and friends.

Phoova – Father's brother-in-law (married to Phoi). So, my husband Peter is Peter Phoova to my nephew and nieces.

Sasu – Mother-in-law.

Sasara – Father-in-law.

Wov – Daughter-in-law.

Jamai – Son-in-law.

NB: For family members and readers who are interested:

There are variable uses of these names, and more complex terms, which can be used to determine the nature of relationships which I have not used; hopefully some readers will know them, others may learn more if they need to.